As from the house your mother sees

You playing round the garden trees

So you may see, if you will look

Through the windows of this book,

Another child, far, far away,

And in another garden, play.

But do not think you can at all,

By knocking on the window, call

That child to hear you. He intent

Is all on his play-business bent.

He does not hear; he will not look,

Nor yet be lured out of this book.

For, long ago, the truth to say,

He has grown up and gone away,

And it is but a child of air

That lingers in the garden there.

Robert Louis Stevenson
A Child's Garden of Verses

MOLLY DANNENMAIER

a child's garden

60 IDEAS TO MAKE ANY GARDEN
COME ALIVE FOR CHILDREN

AN ARCHETYPE PRESS BOOK

TIMBER PRESS

introduction

9   Preface

11   A Child's Garden

18   Child's Play

25   Cultivating Eden

home territories

33   Water Paradise

38   Deck of Delights

44   Jungles' Gym

how children really play

52   **WATER**

54   Musical Fountains

55   Personal Ponds

56   Meandering Brooks

59   Sensational Waterfalls

60   Soothing Pools

63   **CREATURES**

64   Backyard Habitats

65   Fish and Frog Ponds

66   Roosts for Birds

68   Butterfly Ballets

69   Bountiful Bats and Bees

70   Pet Places

72   **REFUGES**

74   Bush and Tree Hideaways

76   Vegetable Bowers

78   Arbor Retreats

79   Miniature Forests

81   Willow Nests

82   Woodland Cottages

87   **DIRT**

88   Earth Berms

89   Digging to China

90   Simple Sandboxes

94   Treasure Hunts

95   Sticks and Stones

97   **HEIGHTS**

98   Trees for Climbing

100   Bewitching Tree Houses

102   Natural Play Structures

103   Magical Beanstalks

104 **MOVEMENT**

106 Indispensable Lawns

108 Soaring Swings

111 Irresistible Slides

112 Ball Tricks

113 Jumping Jacks and Jills

114 Circular Courses

117 **MAKE-BELIEVE**

119 Secret Paths

122 Mesmerizing Mazes

124 Whimsical Espaliers

125 Tempting Topiaries

126 Tall Grasses

128 Spectacular Sunflowers

130 Artful Ornament

132 Poetic Gates

133 Fanciful Fences

134 Playful Peepholes

135 Lilliputian Furniture

136 **NURTURE**

138 Fairy-Tale Vegetables

142 Child-Sized Orchards

143 Candy-Fragrant Herbs

145 Old-Time Berry Bushes

146 Pickable Posies

148 Majestic Meadows

151 **LEARNING**

152 Daunting Dinosaurs

154 Performing Plants

156 Timeless Sundials

158 Easy Alphabets

160 Tinkerbell Gardens

161 Hungry Peter Rabbits

162 Sea Gardens

163 Wizard of Oz Land

164 Earthy Fragrances

166 Family Roots

resources

171 Notes

172 Featured Designers

174 Organizations

175 Children's Gardens

176 Books

177 Illustration Credits

178 Index

introduction

preface

Left: In this "ditch garden" at George Washington's River Farm, Alexandria, Virginia, a child can sit contemplatively on a tiny, grassy bridge made of ash and hazel saplings and dangle her toes in the water. The designer Alastair Bolton used a collection of boughs and a packet of wild-flower seed mix to transform simple things into magic. Above: A welcome sign for the Children's Garden at Longwood Gardens, Kennett Square, Pennsylvania, reminds parents to let children make their own discoveries.

When the first edition of *A Child's Garden* was published, it received an overwhelming response from parents, teachers, and garden designers and administrators who wanted to create environments that reconnected children with the natural world. Yet this relationship has only worsened since then. Childhood obesity has skyrocketed as television and computers and automobile transport have become even more firmly entrenched. As the threat of global climate change demands that we all take care of our planet, getting children back outside seems more essential now than ever before.

While botanical gardens and schools began to embrace the concept of immersing children in the physical world—creating children's gardens that followed the principles of *A Child's Garden*—my family conducted its own experiment in recapturing the natural life. Moving to a village outside Zurich, Switzerland, became a life-changing adventure. We lived without a car—riding bikes and scooters, walking, or taking the train or tram. Our son and daughter made their own way on foot to and from the village school. We bought fresh milk from a local farmer. We tended a lush garden and harvested cherries, grapes, currants, rosemary, and oregano.

Next we moved to cosmopolitan Vienna, Austria, where we rented a villa with mature apple, apricot, and plum trees. We planted a vegetable garden at the bottom of the terraced two-acre yard. Our dinners were filled with food we grew ourselves: fresh lettuces, tomatoes, cucumbers, squash, spinach, and other just-picked delights.

Because their home territory was so inviting, the children chose to spend much of their time in their own back yards. They climbed trees, picked fruit and vegetables, played croquet and badminton, swung, read in the shade, built huts and tepees, and played tag and hide-and-seek with their schoolmates. Their young lives unfolded in such a carefree, natural way. Now we are back in the States, and the good things my children gleaned from their overseas experiences seem to have stayed with them.

It is my hope that this new edition of *A Child's Garden* will offer continuing inspiration to a new generation of parents, educators, designers, and children who desperately need to learn nature's pleasures and lessons. The book looks at what children *really* do when they step outside, unlike what we adults think or wish they might do. The adult-friendly garden ideas presented here show how to create special places in which our children can experience nature—in a way that is true to their own nature—on their own home turf.

a child's garden

To thrive children need complex environments. That much we adults have figured out. And in our attempts to help our children achieve success in an ever more complex world, we try to fill their lives with good things—challenging schooling, enriching extracurricular activities, high-powered computers, developmentally appropriate toys. When our children clamor to go outside, we erect swing sets and slides for them, enroll them in team sports, take them to zoos and adventure parks. But how often do we provide opportunities for our children to deeply explore their own home grounds? How important are the old childhood pleasures of collecting seed pods, fishing in ditches, making bowers, picking flowers, and climbing trees? What should yards have that will be of value to children?

My childhood was spent in a variety of suburban tract houses with parceled-out yards enclosed by chain-link fences. It could have been a sterile existence, but my dad, a farm-raised son of the South, made each yard into something much more than just a space for swing sets and jungle gyms. On evenings and weekends my brothers and sister and I would play outside while our father tended his roses, lilies, strawberry patches, blackberry bushes, fruit trees, and rows of corn, okra, tomatoes, peppers, green beans, carrots, and pumpkins. His diligent presence instilled in each of us a love of gardening. But beyond that, the long hours we whiled away outdoors as he carried out his methodical work offered us the opportunity to explore our wilder natures, to test more primal urges, to be truer to ourselves as children than we were allowed to be indoors.

DISAPPEARING OUTDOOR AFTERNOONS
Long hours of unstructured outdoor exploration are a fast-vanishing aspect of contemporary childhood. Fearing for our children's safety in a more dangerous world than we parents grew up in and frenetically busy with our own lives, many of us today are unwittingly cutting off children from seminal life experiences available only during lazy outdoor afternoons. We promote the idea that the important business of real life happens only in offices and

On their sloping side yard in Glen Echo, Maryland, Holly and Osamu Shimizu created a terraced garden. Alexa Shimizu can now recite its plant names: wild ginger, Solomon's seal, maidenhair fern, and dwarf carex.

Children have an outdoor agenda all their own. Exploratory digging is one of their favorite activities. Adults should set aside space in a family garden for children to dig pits, swales, tunnels, and caves.

classrooms—not in yards, fields, and forests. And in answer to children's inevitable curiosities about nature we offer them books, television shows, and computer learning programs instead of taking them outside to touch, feel, and smell the real thing.

Not so long ago parents and children knew their own outdoor territories intimately. Parents passed on knowledge about useful plants and poisonous ones, safe places and dangerous ones, interesting geological formations and pulsating waterways. But that has changed. Now we worry about the dangers of our children's climbing habits, the study time lost to outdoor play, and the threats of car traffic and strangers—and we tell our children to come inside.

Parents worry that something is wrong with children, especially boys, when they cannot sit still and focused in a classroom for hours at a time deciphering and manipulating symbols. However, scores of studies show that natural environments heighten mental acuity, diminish stress, and even speed physical healing. Sick people who spend time in nature recover more quickly, require less medication and follow-up treatment, and report more interest in work and new projects than patients who do not. People under extreme stress suddenly become calmer in a natural setting: their blood pressure and heart rate drop dramatically while their ability to focus mentally increases. There is even evidence that nature's ever-changing cycles—full of visual, olfactory, and physical complexity—can increase intelligence. People and animals in complex, constantly changing environments show an increase in the number and complexity of the neural connections in their brains: they become smarter. Conversely, creatures in stagnant environments show a decrease in neural complexity: they become both more listless and more violent.

Human beings simply seem wired to work better mentally, physically, and emotionally with steady infusions of nature. Researchers say that this is because we are genetically predisposed to feel most fully at ease in environments that would have facilitated survival for the earliest human ancestors. Wide-open grassy spaces with scattered trees cause children to laugh and run and sing and play. The African savannah, which has exactly these qualities—wide sight lines to keep watch for predators and scattered trees indicating the presence of life-sustaining water—has been shown to be the favored landscape of people in every culture but especially children younger than twelve. Children are inclined to recoil from dark, enclosed spaces where their instincts tell them that predators could easily lurk. Many other human responses—anxiety when confronted with snakes, spiders, and growling animals, pleasure in the presence of verdant vegetation and bubbling water—have been shown to be so constant in every culture, particularly in young children, that researchers presume them to be genetically based.

Young children can offer adults a passage back into a world where intuition reigns supreme, says Charles Lewis, a horticulturist who has spent his career studying human responses to nature. Lewis complains that the last century of scientific advances has led to a society "so dependent on the organizing side of our brain that we've forgotten how legitimate it is to be open to our mind's intuitive responses to the world." But there is a critical timeline for "tuning in" to one's intuition. By the age of twelve, children will have experienced the vast majority of the "biologically prepared learning," in which innate responses to environmental stimuli provoke unforgettable cognitive imprints, says Lewis. So what are the implications when children, generation after generation, receive more "intuition input" during these critical years from the cleanly choreographed, ever captivating, physically nonthreatening worlds of television, computers, and books than from physical experiences in the world of nature itself?

My mother tells me that I first learned to talk at the age of eighteen months during a visit to my uncle's farm in Kentucky. The environment there, which I would visit time and again throughout my growing-up years, was so complex—full of smells, varied land forms, and mesmerizing creatures. I remember a scooped-out pond surrounded by mud in which pigs, ducks, and geese joyously wallowed. The strange pungency of the air, the frighteningly gigantic hogs, the mysterious, billowy grasses, the ancient wells and water pumps, barns and outbuildings, and varied fences in different states of repair still fill my senses. Obviously there was much to talk about!

CHILDREN'S GARDENS PAST

What is the best outdoor environment for children? Is it one in which they climb on exercise equipment or cavort in gardens, play with prefabricated toys or hunt for natural treasures, spend all afternoon swinging or care for animals? Is it one in which they have freedom to explore or are guided by adults? Such questions arose in nineteenth-century Europe as industrialization swept families away from the countryside and into crowded cities.

German educators and social reformers of the time were among the first to create children's playgrounds. They did so in the belief that city children suffered physically, intellectually, and morally when deprived of the riches of

A scented butterfly garden attracts more than just winged visitors to its brilliant blooms. Watkins Elementary School in Washington, D.C., uses easy-to-grow Mexican sunflowers, cosmos, zinnias, and celosia.

In the early twentieth century William Robertson Coe, an insurance executive, had this fully functional pink stucco cottage built as the centerpiece of his daughter Natalie's garden on their 409-acre estate, Planting Fields, in Oyster Bay, New York.

outdoor life so accessible to children in the country. (Remember the story of Heidi?) Friedrich Froebel, the German educator who invented the first kindergarten—literally "garden of children"—in 1837, promoted the idea that young children's play yards should distill the most edifying aspects of country life. Froebel's kindergarten yards were filled with plants, animals, building materials, simple props, and well-trained teachers who guided children through experiential lessons in the physical world. On Froebel's heels in the 1880s, German social reformers created the first public children's "sand gardens" by placing heaps of sand in public parks in Berlin. Such models—in which urban children had opportunities to garden, care for animals, explore nature, build their own creations, and play in sand—began sprouting copies in cities throughout the world.

But by the early twentieth century the outdoor play movement had turned a different corner. Exercise equipment from industrial-sized swings to slides and jungle gyms became the primary focus. Hundreds of iron-and-steel playgrounds were erected in U.S. cities between 1905 and 1909. Manufactured equipment soon began to dominate all landscapes for children, not just in cities but even, as the century progressed, in the most rural schoolyards, parks, and eventually backyards. The earlier goal of creating naturalistic play yards for urban children had been turned on its head. Now even rural children—those closest to nature—were led to believe that the best places for play were made of metal and concrete.

At the same time that mass-produced equipment was becoming ubiquitous, wealthy Americans were taking a more traditional European approach to their own children's outdoor play. On early-twentieth-century estates the centerpiece of the children's garden was often a multiroom outdoor playhouse in English country, American rustic, Gothic Revival, or mock Tudor style. These fantasy playhouses with tiny, custom-made furniture inside were surrounded by manicured gardens, wildflower meadows, and cleared woods and quite possibly were influenced by the examples laid out in 1908 by the renowned English landscape designer Gertrude Jekyll in her classic book *Children and Gardens.*

Jekyll recommended that parents offer children a full-scale outdoor playhouse with a kitchen, parlor, pantry, screened porch, fireplace, and working cookstove in which they could practice all aspects of the domestic arts. Jekyll prescribed surrounding gardens with a wide variety of vegetables and flowers that adults should plant and children should learn to tend, harvest, and prepare in the playhouse kitchen for afternoon teas. Many of Jekyll's suggestions are both charming and useful, such as her advice on which tools children should keep and how to use and store them—a "spade, rake, hoe, a little wooden trug-basket, and a blunt weeding knife; a good cutting knife, a trowel, a hand-fork, and a little barrow," to be used equally with both hands for "general dexterity and convenience" and never put away dirty. But if her ideal of the playhouse as a fully functional replica of an adult house seems somewhat excessive today, it must have seemed even more so in her day, when only the wealthiest families could have chosen such an option for their children. Yet such fantastically unattainable landscapes are the ones history has preserved as examples of "children's gardens." No wonder many parents are skeptical of their ability to replicate one in the backyard.

In the late nineteenth century the Green Animals Topiary Garden in Portsmouth, Rhode Island—three acres of California privet, English boxwood, and yew shrubs clipped to resemble camels, birds, teddy bears, overstuffed chairs, spirals, and other whimsical forms—was created by Joseph Carreiro, the Portuguese gardener for the industrialist Thomas Brayton. Green Animals was never intended as a children's garden, although since it was opened to the public in the 1970s children have flocked to it, inflicting great damage on its hundred-year-old shrubs by attempting to interact with what they see as giant green toys. The topiaries of Green Animals have inspired children's garden displays in public gardens for decades. But such "look-but-don't-touch" gardens are better suited for adults than children, who will always want to touch what appeals to them.

The Brooklyn Botanic Garden's Children's Garden, established in 1914 as the first public teaching garden in the United States, has always offered children the opportunity to touch as well as to learn the skills and discipline of the agricultural arts. It was designed with rows on rows of five-by-seven-foot garden beds to be planted, tended, and harvested by teams of school-age "garden partners" working on afternoons and weekends, and it has been enormously popular. The teaching garden continues to draw nature-starved children from New York City to its verdant plots and has inspired the establishment of other such gardens nationwide.

Victory gardens in American backyards during World War II firmly established the idea in many people's minds that the best garden for children was a utilitarian one, where lessons about industry, thrift, and nurture could be learned through the tilling of practical plots. But as the war years gave way

Gertrude Jekyll regarded the garden as both a delight for children's senses and an opportunity to develop horticultural and domestic skills. In *Children and Gardens,* she showed how to prepare playhouse tea with fresh cress for sandwiches and chamomile to drink.

to the prosperous 1950s, a new backyard philosophy began to emerge. Landscape designers such as Thomas Church in California created a new aesthetic for outdoor living that stressed low-maintenance plantings chosen to withstand the neglect of busy families and large paved and decked areas for outdoor relaxing, entertaining, and children's play. For Church and his disciples, the garden became "an informal outdoor living room filled with deck chairs, tables, and swings, more social than horticultural in its intention." One legacy of this low-maintenance philosophy, visionary as it was at its inception, has been the proliferation of American yards devoid of complexity. Most families now follow a fairly standard formula: shrubs and flowers around the house's foundation, a grassy yard speckled with a few trees, a deck or patio for outdoor meals, and a swing or climbing set for the children. Yet so much more than this is possible.

Today, more than one hundred fifty years after the outdoor ideals of "kindergarten" were first articulated, children's gardens for play are finally beginning to sprout anew in public gardens, museums, schoolyards, hospitals, and parks across the United States. In these places a new generation of children is discovering the joys of outdoor play in miniature forests, dinosaur gardens, and bat caves. Some of the children's gardens to which parents can look for examples to emulate on their own soil include the Brooklyn Botanic Garden in New York, home to the venerable children's garden that has opened an innovative discovery section; the Michigan 4-H Children's Garden at Michigan State University in East Lansing, whose sixty theme gardens make it among the most creative American children's playscapes; Longwood Gardens in Kennett Square, Pennsylvania, with one of the first interactive children's landscapes in the United States; George Washington's River Farm in Alexandria, Virginia, administered by the American Horticultural Society, a rich complex with ten children's demonstration gardens; the Phipps Conservatory in Pittsburgh, Pennsylvania, a new interactive garden with water features, a maze, and a gigantic tree-stump lookout; and the expansive New York Botanical Garden in the Bronx, which provides teaching plots that local children cultivate throughout the year as well as a Family Garden adventure area. The Botanical Garden's new Everett Children's Adventure Garden is the largest and most comprehensive children's landscape in the United States—eight acres for learning and play.

At the close of a century dominated by manufacturing and technology, people have become hungry for ways to reembrace nature. And the garden is again emerging as one of the most compelling outdoor play spaces that adults can create for children.

Early in the twentieth century gardens came to be associated with hard work, and stripped landscapes dominated children's play. Opposite, top: Young World War I–era New Yorkers tend the Avenue A Children's Garden. Bottom: Lenox Hill residents test out a modern iron-and-steel playground in 1928. Above: Now the garden, in places such as the New York Botanical Garden's Family Garden, is being reinvented as a place for children to play.

c h i l d ' s   p l a y

How do children *really* play outside when adults let them do what they want to do? What outdoor elements are inherently captivating to children? Like children's literature and films, the best children's gardens are those that appeal as much to parents as to their offspring because they touch some universal chord born in childhood. In other words, the best children's gardens will always be places that parents can fully enjoy too.

That said, a child's garden should definitely not be designed around adult preferences. Adults love fragrant plots and viewing gardens, planned to delight the olfactory and visual nerves but not intended to be climbed into, picked with abandon, and rolled around in. A child's garden should be a place where children are allowed to run, play, climb, and freely experience natural materials and bodily sensations. Flowers and berries for picking can be planted in exuberant swaths, with paths made perhaps of yellow bricks winding through their beds. Climbing trees and hiding bushes should camouflage every corner. Miniature forests and meadows can be planted, miniature hills mounded, places for digging and constructing set aside. Rabbit hutches and doghouses should be designed with whimsical flair instead of utilitarian drudge. And water is essential—it is children's (not to mention adults') favorite outdoor feature.

ELEMENTAL CONSIDERATIONS

The following nine elements and activities outline how children really play and thrive in the out-of-doors. They also form the groups of examples that make up the heart of the book. There, in part two, are five dozen simple ideas for implementing these basic themes in any garden.

WATER . The eloquent Washington, D.C., garden writer Henry Mitchell once said that probably "the greatest physical joy available to a mortal (over the years and all things considered) is to slop about with water and to stay within sight of it at all times." Even the smallest city garden can accommodate a fountain or a small pool to feed children's primal need to see, hear, and feel water's clear, cool essence.

A garden for child's play leaves room for imagination. A big orange pumpkin becomes a coach for a princess. A gargantuan leaf hides the antics of a winged fairy. A tiny pumpkin is a gift for an invisible playmate.

Children love the shivery sensation of holding crawly creatures. A gardener's best friend, the earthworm, helps enrich garden soil by creating airy tunnels into which young plants can stretch their roots, leaving behind nutrient-rich castings.

CREATURES. Children are captivated by living faces. They love to touch animals far more than any inanimate object (plants included, alas). Petting zoos figured this out a long time ago. Environmentally sensitive backyard gardens will attract wild visitors. And artfully designed pet houses can enhance a garden's appeal to both adults and children.

REFUGES. One of the most universal activities of childhood is to create caves, houses, dens, and fortresses from found materials. All people, children in particular, seek out nestlike places that provide complete camouflage but that offer some "window" to keep watch for predators. Playhouses, willow nests, vegetable bowers, and miniature forests can all serve as safe, mysterious children's havens.

DIRT. Dirt, sand, sticks, and stones are articles that many parents are loathe to let their children experiment with outside. But according to playground theorists, these "loose parts" of nature are among children's favorite things. They are the raw materials through which children can create outdoor worlds from their own imaginations—instead of relying on slick, adult-conceived prefabricated playthings.

HEIGHTS. Children love to survey a terrain from the highest point they can find. Climbing to the top of a mountain, traversing the winding stairs of a castle, shooting up the bullet elevator of a skyscraper—ascending to the top of something tall is a thrill. Children's gardens should have climbing trees, tree houses, or rooftop perches to satisfy this need to be on the top of their world.

MOVEMENT. Children are joyfully physical beings, far more so than adults. They love to run, twirl, dance, jump, slide, swing, and roll down hills, usually laughing and screaming all the while. Parents need to make room mentally and physically for children to move. Grassy play areas, winding pathways, and places for jumping all fill the bill.

MAKE-BELIEVE. Trying on a variety of roles is the most important work of childhood. Only through play can children visualize themselves as the adventurers, explorers, nurturers, discoverers, and artists they will eventually become. Landscapes where whimsical images greet children at various turns can fuel their creative play even further. Imagine turning a corner to be

greeted by a tree growing in the shape of a heart or finding a maze that leads to a secret nest. Adults should pepper outdoor spaces with such surprises.

NURTURE. Children can learn to take care of their own outdoor patch of the world, but usually only with subtle, clear-sighted guidance from an adult. Planting spaces can range from containers on balconies or decks, to rectangular plots in a yard, to free-range seed scattered throughout an entire outdoor space. Pickable flowers, thornless berries, and miniature vegetables are highly child-friendly choices.

Water is given its due in a family garden in Phoenix, designed by Steve Martino. This bubbling, tiled oasis offers a splashy counterpoint to the native desert plantings on the hillside just beyond the walled patio.

Openness and enclosure each
have a place in a child's garden.
Above: A grassy lawn offers
a sweet spot for thinking.
Right: A kousa dogwood arbor
provides a private nook.

LEARNING. Children are constantly learning even when they think they are just having fun. Theme gardens with plants related to something that holds a particular fascination for children can seduce them into hours of self-propelled nature study. A garden of plants that flourished during the age of dinosaurs, a Jack and the Beanstalk garden of quick-vining beans, a planted area based on a town or community's own local history, or an alphabet garden—from A (for aster) to Z (for zinnia)—can teach even the youngest children lessons based on real physical experiences.

GATEWAYS BACK TO NATURE

Young children use the natural environment to become familiar with the mechanics of their own bodies. As they grow, nature serves as a science lab cum theater where they test out principles about the world their bodies inhabit. When large numbers of children cease to experience physical learning outdoors in the informality of their own home territory, what does it mean for society as a whole?

Most children today no longer know the names, uses, and histories of the plants, animals, landmarks, and waterways that surround their homes. And schoolyards, the last truly communal outdoor spaces available to young people, often lack botanical complexity, many having been stripped, asphalted, and furnished with chain-link fences and play equipment that is sterile if not dangerous to their health and welfare.

If it is true that to care deeply about nature as adults, people must have intimate experiences with nature as children, then the world community faces a huge problem. Humankind's next great challenge will be to devise new ways to preserve and reconstruct the earth's natural systems, although the natural experiences that previously informed every aspect of childhood have been allowed to become nearly extinct.

But parents, grandparents, and other adults can change this—if we tap into children's innate enthusiasm about the natural world as a way of rekindling our own. Together with children we can investigate our neighborhood's social and natural history and its botanical and geological mysteries. We can look to knowledgeable sources: books, maps, animal and plant identification guides, and neighborhood elders to learn unknown names and stories. We can visit children's gardens for more ideas. And then, with all this newfound knowledge and reignited awe, we can create Eden anew—in our own backyards.

Unexpected pleasures are still the best. The pliant, inviting texture of moist grass, the ripping sensation when roots separate from earth, the mingled smells of soil, dew, and vegetation—all these make an imprint on a child's heart.

cultivating eden

Reconciling adults' and children's outdoor needs requires planning. Adults' minds and bodies are simply different from children's. Adults are more cerebral, children more physical. Although their paths certainly cross, they generally do not overlap for long stretches. Parents should not be frustrated when children tire of the family catnip planting project in five minutes and abandon it to chase the cat.

Some parents simply forgo the idea of having an outdoor room of their own for a decade or so while young children, with all their plastic play accoutrements, rule the backyard roost. Others create gardens but attempt to keep children out instead of inviting them in. A successful family garden, however, is one where neither the adults' nor the children's needs dominate the other. Adults and children do not have to be engaged in the same activity to spend satisfying outdoor time in close proximity. To get along well with each other outside, parents must allow children to be themselves, and children must learn that parents have their own, very different requirements. So how can children's desire for a space in which to trample, dig, build forts, and play with animals be reconciled with adults' need for the peace and solace that only a personalized patch of nature can bring? The answer is to claim separate territories while remaining within each other's purview.

Ideal "grown-up" spaces for gardening and relaxing offer a peaceful reprieve while providing clear visual access to children's activities. Terraces, patios, and seating throughout the garden are highly important elements for adults. Plants well loved by parents should be protected by family rules as well as by stone walls, hedge borders, tough informal shrubs, or sturdy pots.

For children two requirements are crucial: a place for freedom of movement and a place for privacy. A grassy lawn space or a mulch-covered running area is important for games and acrobatics. In more private areas created by shrub barriers, weeping trees, or outdoor architecture, children can feel hidden but know that they are just steps away from a parent's comforting watchfulness.

Adults and children usually like to engage in different activities when they are outdoors. Adults often enjoy the meditative aspects of weeding, pruning, and watering. Most children like to dig, stomp, run, and splash. But the garden can offer special moments where the generations come together.

In this hidden spot at the American Christmas Museum, Chadd's Ford, Pennsylvania, evergreen trees create a wall of privacy from adults, a tiny playhouse and a beanpole tepee offer places to hide, and a scarecrow topiary covered with creeping nasturtium becomes an imaginary playmate.

CHILD-FRIENDLY LANDSCAPING

One simple truth is that when children play outdoors they make a mess. Some parents keep scrap lumber and rope on their property for child-initiated construction projects, while others carve out relatively large unturfed spaces where children can dig pits, swales, and caves. Children's own creative junkyards, offbeat planting plots, and "outdoor museums" further litter backyard landscapes.

CAMOUFLAGING THE PLAYSCAPE. A screen of plant materials can mask children's activities while allowing freedom to engage in them. Screens can be created by raised beds of tough, tall perennials or a wall of grasses or informal shrubs. Tall grasses could include such beauties as feather reed grass, pampas grass, and fountain grass. Abelia, weigela, viburnum, photinia, arborvitae, and willow make good shrub barriers that still can be seen through.

TOUGH PLANTS FOR TRAMPLING TOES. Children can be hard on plants, but many commonly known and loved plants can withstand just about anything that kids—and their animals—can dish out. Tough woody plants and herbaceous perennials can be planted at the edges of backyard ball-playing areas, around playhouses, and along pathways. Buddleia, pampas grass, mallow, periwinkle, lamb's ears, lady's mantle, cotoneaster, woolly thyme, sandwort, harebell, and snow-in-summer all stand up well to abuse.

SAFETY IN THE GARDEN

When I was a child, children did not wear helmets while riding bicycles, playgrounds had lots of big swing sets, and backyards and vacant lots were filled with renegade tree houses. Today helmets are often required by law, swing sets are liabilities, and tree-house construction is governed by strict local building codes. There is nothing wrong with trying to keep children safe, but the environment with the least possibility of physical risk is not necessarily the best one for them. Learning to distinguish between prudent and foolish risk is a basic lesson of life that parents must teach their children.

Children can be both tender and tough toward garden plants. Parents should carry out simple tasks, such as watering, and offer children the opportunity to help. Performed regularly, such small rituals pave the way for more responsibility.

CREATURES. A backyard habitat garden, for example, will just as likely attract rats, mice, and bats as squirrels, opossums, and herons. Any of these animals, if provoked, might bite. Should parents thus not try to create backyard habitats? Or could adults and children use this as an opportunity to learn how to safely approach and observe wildlife?

For a child who is extremely allergic to bee stings, instead of eliminating all plant materials from the yard, parents might simply eliminate flowering plants, which attract bees. A garden of nonflowering plants, many of which have survived since prehistoric times, can recreate in a small way the landscape of the dinosaurs.

TOXIC PLANTS. Some of the most common garden plants have parts that are extremely toxic, including morning glory (its seeds), yew (its leaves and seeds), and foxglove (all parts). Should parents thus never include poisonous plants in a garden for children? Or do such plants present an opportunity for learning botanical lessons and setting backyard rules?

Although children's deaths from garden plant poisoning are rare, a number of the most common garden plants can be fatal if ingested in large

Above left: A wall of tall, tough feather reed grass can create a see-through screen to camouflage children's outdoor messes while offering a sense of privacy. Right: Soft lamb's ears are among children's favorite garden plants, and they are one of the toughest as well, standing up to acrobatic accidents, ball pummeling, and scampering pet feet.

enough quantities. Some, such as the castor-bean seed, can kill a child who eats even one of them. Many plants have parts that are poisonous, such as the bulb (amaryllis and daffodil), leaves (apple and privet), seeds (apple and wisteria), berries (holly and privet), and pods (wisteria). All parts of some other common plants are poisonous, including anemone, caladium, foxglove, hydrangea, lantana, mistletoe, and philodendron. Obviously, it would be nearly impossible to ban all toxic plants from family gardens. Most children older than three will immediately spit out natural poisons because they usually taste so terrible. But it is crucial to be aware of the toxicity of every plant that grows in the yard.

A THORNY ISSUE. One might recommend that plants with thorns and prickers never be included in a child's garden. Why, after all, subject children to unnecessary splinters and scratches? But thorny plants can play a highly important role: protecting children from entering dangerous areas. A dense row of thorny shrubs may be just as effective as a fence in keeping a child from wandering into septic fields, off cliffs, and into electrical hazards. Natural alternatives to barbed wire include five-leafed aralia, barberry, thorny elaeagnus, scarlet fire thorn, flowering quince, and rugosa rose.

DANGEROUS HEIGHTS. Sometimes children who climb trees fall out of them. Should parents forbid children to climb trees? Or should they find ways to accommodate children's natural urge to climb? Lower tree limbs can be left to grow unpruned, and the ground beneath climbing trees can be covered with wood chips or pine needles to help break falls. Rather than rejecting the idea of a tree house, parents can study local building codes and work with the child to build one.

Hazards are different from challenges. The environmental playground designers Robin C. Moore, Susan Goltsman, and Daniel Iacofano define a hazard as "something a child does not see," a challenge as "a risk the child can see and chooses to undertake or not." The safety philosophy I espouse is that hazards should be avoided and risks should be explored—cautiously. Examples throughout this book show how different families deal with potentially dangerous garden features. Each family should arm itself with as much knowledge as possible about garden safety issues and set its own outdoor rules.

As busy as parents are, they must not simply shield children from dangers but teach them how to play—and live—as safely as possible. The attitude that dangers must be avoided at all costs will lead children to a distorted view of the natural world.

Above left: Many of the most common garden plants—including all varieties of daffodil—have parts that are poisonous, in this case the bulb. Rather than banning toxic plants, parents can use them to teach children valuable lessons. Right: Barberries and other thorny bushes work as well as fences in keeping children from going into a hazardous or private area.

home territories

I CALLED THE LITTLE POOL A SEA;

When Holly and Osamu Shimizu, both horticulturists, moved into their Glen Echo, Maryland, house in 1986, the sloping quarter-acre lot had a chain-link fence, patchy grass, and a few mature trees. But within two years the couple had transformed the space into an unorthodox family garden where sophisticated Eastern and Western garden styles merge with rubber ducks, a hidden fort, and a Tarzan-style zip wire strung diagonally across a dark, formal pool. The impact of this garden on their two young children, Bevan and Alexa, who were four and one when it was completed, "has been immeasurable," says Holly. "Our life as a family has been one hundred times better than it would have been otherwise."

The Shimizus have made the most of their outdoor space, creating five distinct garden rooms: a sunken lawn and an herb garden in the front, a shady meditation garden in the southeast corner, a textured terrace garden on the east side, and a moss garden in the rear northeast corner. But the crowning achievement of the multifaceted yard is the densely planted rock and water garden in the back. This thirty-by-fifty-foot space—which from a child's perspective resembles a miniature mountain with a stream running down to a darkly inviting lake—is the Shimizu children's most beloved territory.

The water garden's most stunning—and potentially most dangerous—feature is its twenty-five by sixteen-foot pool, three feet deep and lined with black rubber. This is the terminus of the built stream that begins in the rear northwest corner of the yard and meanders down a lush rocky hillside created from the soil and rubble excavated during the digging of the pool. About two-thirds of the way down the hill the stream widens and drops from a tiny waterfall into a one-foot-deep, seven-foot-wide pond. From here it spills over a flagstone shelf, creating a crashing two-foot waterfall, and ends in the formal, rectangular pool, bordered by a mosaiclike fieldstone and black pebble walk.

Around the water garden the Shimizus have planted some seventy plant varieties. Woody plants include Korean boxwood, dwarf Japanese black

The lower waterfall plunges into the pool, a dramatic culmination of the built stream system in the Shimizu garden. The pool is only three feet deep—ten-year-old Bevan can sit on the bottom—but allows for plenty of fun and exercise. Plants around the waterfall include a red cut-leaf Japanese maple (right), a dwarf red pine (left), winter jasmine, and variegated glacier ivy.

From the Shimizu family's **house (A)**, glass doors lead directly onto a **deck (B)**, where the children grow their own herbs, flowers, and vegetables in containers. The narrow **front lawn (C)**, bordered by fragrant herbs, is used by the children for soccer games and acrobatics. The **meditation garden (D)**, in the lawn's front corner, has as its center a three-tiered Victorian fountain and, just beyond its evergreen walls, a bench facing the parents' **terraced side garden (E)**, filled with plants of exotic texture, color, and fragrance. The **moss lawn (F)** is bordered by the children's favorite hiding foliage: blue Atlas cedar, acuba, and Foster hollies. The **pool (G)** is the culmination of all the water elements—the **larger waterfall (H)**, a shallow **pond (I)**, a **small waterfall (J)**, and the **stream (K)**. The children's **wooden fort and walkway (L)** are tucked behind trees in the yard's rear northwest corner.

Opposite, clockwise from top left: Bevan's box garden includes the ingredients for tasty homemade pizza: tomatoes, basil, oregano, and peppers. The Shimizu children's tree fort is screened by trees. Alexa and a friend prepare tea around the Victorian fountain. A painted sign shows how seriously the children care for their garden.

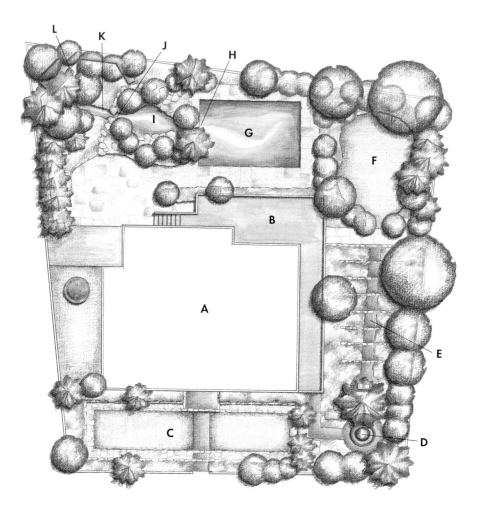

pine, and Carolina cherry. The ground covers that inch their way around the hillside's rocks include a glossy native ginger, soft lamb's ears, dwarf nandina, winter jasmine, and variegated ivy.

Although the Shimizu children have free run of the entire yard—on the sunken lawn in front they play soccer with their friends, and at the base of the moss garden they stake out spaces behind the blue Atlas cedar, acuba, and Foster hollies for hiding games—their presence does not overpower the garden. When the play equipment is stowed under the house at the end of the day, the yard becomes the most aesthetically pleasing of adult gardens. At night the delicate, melodic sounds of the stream and the rushing of the waterfall "make us feel that we are in a very cool, very far-away place," says Holly. "Instead of having to drive out to the country, all we've ever had to do to feel like we're escaping the city is walk into our own backyard."

I SEARCHED THE CAVERNS UP AND DOWN, AND NAMED THEM ONE AND ALL. **3 5**

I PLAYED THERE WERE NO DEEPER SEAS,

The Shimizus made their small backyard seem vast by forgoing a lawn and building a miniature mountain, a stream, two waterfalls, a pond, and a naturalistic pool. Then they filled the space with diverse foliage—more than seventy plant varieties chosen for the shape, color, and texture of their leaves. "Alexa will stay out there literally eight hours straight, and you couldn't distract her from it," says her mother, Holly Shimizu.

deck of delights

It is June, and the Santa Barbara landscape architect Isabelle Greene, grand-daughter of the consummate Arts and Crafts architect Henry Mather Greene, is conducting research along with her associate Yvonne Chin: they swoosh down slides in children's parks, shoot down escape poles in fire stations, and study the refracting capacity of antique glass prisms used in old whaling ships to allow natural light to illuminate the lower decks. By September, Greene's clients, Don and Mary Lou Crocker, are enjoying the fruits of this intensive labor—a new children's garden with an ingeniously terraced, three-tiered redwood deck for their Rincon Beach house in Carpinteria, California.

The two-story, wood-shingled cottage was built by Don Crocker's parents in the 1940s. After sustaining heavy water damage during a storm in the early 1990s, it was redesigned and raised on stilts. The back of the house, now a half story above ground level, has been transformed by the deck, which over-looks a sloping, grassy yard and, beyond a trellis fence, a slough wetlands preserve and the mountains north of Santa Barbara.

A place for adults to relax and socialize, the deck is also an unforget-table play space for the Crockers' eleven grandchildren. Tucked in the corner against the house is an Art Nouveau—style slide made of brass, steel, copper, and bronze that offers a thrilling fifteen-foot ride to the ground. A brass pole just like a firefighter's allows children to twirl two and one-half stories down to a sandy landing. Antique hexagonal, six-inch-wide glass prisms line the deck's upper perimeters, serving as miniature skylights for the playing area underneath. And curvilinear railings made of brass, copper, and bronze connect one section of the deck to another and impart a sense of organic fluidity to this atypical structure. "It's an adventure maze for our grandchildren," says Don Crocker, "but it's also an aesthetic delight for us."

The deck serves additionally as a shady roof under which the children can seek refuge from the hot summer sun without having to take their play indoors. The glass prisms in the floors of the upper deck allow refracted light

The Crocker deck serves as an adventure maze for eleven grandchildren. At every bend another surprise awaits. Here a grandchild pops his head out of a porthole from a secret hiding chamber nestled between the redwood deck's two main levels. To the right a brass, steel, copper, and bronze Art Nouveau sliding board offers a quick commute to the ground.

ALL MADE OF THE BACK-BEDROOM CHAIRS,

Above and right: The Crocker
grandchildren can choose from
an array of devices for getting
from the top of the deck down
to the yard, two and one-half
stories below—a brass firefighter's pole, a sinuous slide, or
a set of swirling redwood stairs.

Left: The deck serves as a promontory for taking in views beyond the property: a slough wetlands preserve and the mountains north of Santa Barbara. Above: Antique glass prisms used to illuminate lower decks of old whaling ships line the deck's perimeter, allowing sunlight to shine into the sheltered play space below.

An aged pepper tree on the property's back corner is perfect for climbing. The small yard has a meadowy feel, thanks to an undulating border of sedge grasses and tough perennials that can withstand rough games.

to shine down on the children as they play. "The filtered light from above makes it seem like another world down there," says Greene. At night the prisms continue to refract light, but upward instead of downward. Lamps installed under them bring glowing light back up onto the upper deck areas.

A wood trellis fence, overgrown with climbing roses, wisteria, clematis, and potato vine, offers a surprisingly agreeable eighteen-foot-tall separation between the Crockers and their next-door neighbors. The fence stairsteps down as it reaches into the yard, where less height is needed. The salt-water-and-sand-tolerant lawn is planted with Excalibur Burmuda grass, whose roots go down twelve feet to hold the sand if water comes in over it. The lawn is bordered by a billowing edge of sedge grasses and blooming perennials that create a meadowy effect.

This unusually complex project had unusual rewards. "All of us adults had to try out all the children's equipment throughout the installation process—to test safety, of course," Greene says. "I must say that we all found this remarkably fun."

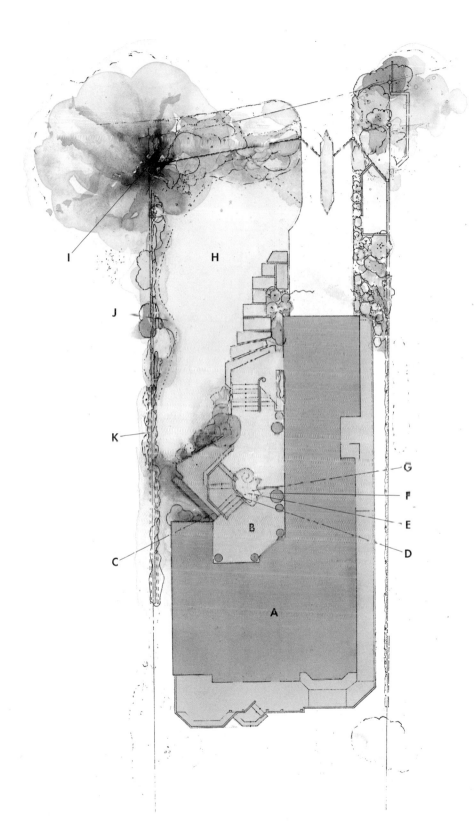

From the top floor of the **house (A)**, the Crocker grandchildren can open doors onto the **three-tiered redwood deck (B),** which is a focal point for fun. There they find three alternatives for getting to the ground: an Art-Nouveau–style **slide (C)**, a set of curving **steps (D)** lined with antique glass prisms, and a brass firefighter's **pole (E).** Once they reach the ground, an **under-deck play area (F)**, illuminated by natural light filtered through the glass prisms, offers refuge from the sun. On the way down the children can take a detour into a **secret hiding chamber (G)** with a porthole window between the deck's upper and lower levels. At ground level they can move out onto the **lawn (H)** for games or acrobatics. A fifty-year-old **pepper tree (I)** in the yard's back corner is perfect for climbing. The billowing **border plantings (J)** of tough sedge grasses and perennials can withstand the abuse of stray balls. The wood trellis **privacy fence (K),** covered with climbing roses, wisteria, clematis, and potato vine, is eighteen feet tall at its highest point and stair-steps down as it stretches into the yard.

j u n g l e s ' g y m

In the small Florida garden that the landscape architect Raymond Jungles and the artist Debra Yates share with their children, nine and eleven, it is sometimes hard to tell just whose childhood is unfolding here. On languid afternoons an unannounced visitor might be as likely to find mother and father in the tree house as daughter and son. At night Yates and Jungles enjoy leading a band of neighborhood children with flashlights through garden foliage in search of sleeping lizards and grasshoppers.

The Jungles-Yates garden, a 125-by-150-foot tropical enclosure just outside Coconut Grove, is a sophisticated mix of tropical plants and ceramic mosaic murals that recalls the designs of the couple's mentor and friend, the late Roberto Burle Marx, the legendary Brazilian artist and garden designer. Jungles sculpts spaces with bold arrangements of palms, cycads, bromeliads, tropical vines, and citrus and banana trees. Yates creates brilliantly colorful abstract tile murals that serve as garden walls.

But artfully hidden in the cracks and crevices of this garden's many outdoor rooms is one special place after another designed just for children. A trapeze hangs from a twenty-foot-high branch of a mature mango tree just beyond the luminous swimming pool. Secluded under the shade of palms is a seven-by-ten-foot sandlot. A tree house fifteen feet above the ground, painted a dark gray-green, disappears into the branches of a fiddle-leaf fig. Vibrant paints have transformed a 1970s-vintage wooden climbing structure into an African-striped artwork. Just beside it stands a mature grapefruit tree, perfect for climbing. A basketball hoop with a clear backstop fades into the foliage of the surrounding orchid and palm trees. And a forty-by-twenty-foot playing field, named "Jungles' stadium" by the children, is covered in pine needles and bordered by a lush blend of practically indestructible plants, including a frangipani tree, a native Jamaican caper shrub, and a set of piccabeen palms.

Both parents remember having a great deal of freedom outdoors when they were growing up and want to recreate a sense of that for their own

A tropical garden designed around the artistic sensibilities of the parents holds one special place after another for the children, camouflaged by bold foliage. Here a trapeze swings from the branch of a mango tree. When not in use, its blue and green ropes fade into the surrounding fronds. A seven-by-ten-foot sandlot rests in the shade of palms just beyond.

OH, I DO THINK IT THE PLEASANTEST THING EVER A CHILD CAN DO!

Raymond Jungles took a couple of days off work and built this tree house for his children, Benjamin and Amanda, without a blueprint. "I like to work out of my head," he says. He painted the structure dark gray-green to blend into the foliage of the fiddle-leaf fig that holds it. An old radio tower ladder offers access up. Mother and father enjoy spending time here as much as the children do.

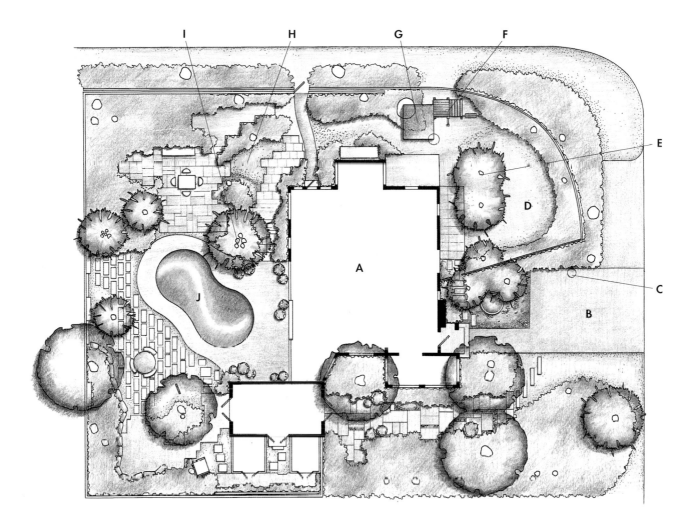

children. Yates recalls spending long days playing and hiding in the seclusion of sea hibiscus trees overgrown with morning glories in the unbuilt lot next to her family's home in Key West. Jungles, who lived in towns from California to Illinois during his childhood, delighted in catching horned toads and lizards in culverts, playing hooky from school to catch crawdads in the park all day with his brother, building a deep cave with a buddy, swinging on vines in neighborhood "forests," and constructing his own tree house out of two-by-fours and plywood, all before the age of nine.

The Jungles-Yates family garden offers, in one small way, freedom of exploration and that most important of childhood commodities: intimate knowledge of every crack and crevice. "I think the greatest thing parents can do for their children is expose them to nature," says Jungles. "It's those early ages when you really are receptive that you can develop a love for it—but only if you get to know it."

In the Jungles-Yates garden, spaces are always evolving. In front of the **house (A)**, a one-time parking pad has become a **patio–basketball court (B)** with a clear Plexiglas **backboard (C)**. In the mulched yard of **"Jungles' stadium" (D)**, the children play games and climb the mature **grapefruit tree (E)**. The side yard contains an African-painted **play structure (F)** and a **tree house (G)**. In the backyard the children may dig in a shady **sandlot (H)**, hang from a **trapeze (I)**, and swim in the **pool (J)**.

Right above: After visiting the Costa Rican rainforest during a family vacation, the Jungles kids learned that creatures of all types sleep right out on the leaves of tropical plants after the sun sets. The family now leads flashlight-wielding bands of neighborhood children through the garden after dark on hunts for sleeping grasshoppers and lizards. All around, dangerous plants fill the garden floor, including toxic caladiums and prickly cycads. "We've taught the children right from the start about the properties of these plants," says Yates. "They've respected the danger." Below: Amanda rests after a day of swinging and climbing in her own paradise. Opposite: Yates and the children transformed a weary old climbing structure that a neighbor had put out for the garbage collector. Bold paints, a new swing, and a shady spot in the garden brought it back to life.

UP IN THE AIR I GO FLYING AGAIN, UP IN THE AIR AND DOWN!

how children really play

w a t e r

The urge to seek water is one of the deepest human drives. Whenever children step outdoors, they seem to have an extrasensory ability to find water in any form—alley puddles, gutter streams, ditches, ponds teeming with tadpoles. Being near water reduces a person's heart rate, respiration, and blood pressure. Water's soothing presence makes thoughts seem clearer, children sweeter, responsibilities lighter. In addition to its calming influence, water seems to heighten the senses. But when it comes to pairing up children and water in the garden, red lights start flashing for many parents. Children may get dirty, wet, cold, or sick; they may even drown. Clearly, safety is an issue that cannot be overemphasized. Young children must always be supervised near outdoor pools and ponds because they can drown in as little as two inches of water. For this reason many parents do not include permanent water features in their gardens, choosing instead to drape hoses over lawn chairs and to place plastic wading pools on patios. But these are not the only safe alternatives. With a little imagination fountains, ponds, streams, waterfalls, and pools—and clear safety procedures—can all be part of a family garden.

This lily pond at George Washington's River Farm is only eighteen inches deep, but its spouting fountain and dramatic, oversized plants make it a magical experience for a child.

A fountain is a good first step for families new to water gardening. It takes up a minimum of space but still provides soothing music and a place for children to splash. Fountain mechanics are simple: A submersible electric pump placed in a catch basin pushes water up through a plastic tube. At the top the water is released, to spill back down into the basin.

The tube that carries the water up can be adorned in any number of artistic ways, from Victorian cast iron to modern cast concrete. For the catch basin anything impermeable and deep enough to hold eighteen or so inches of recirculating water will do— a mortared in-ground reservoir, a metal cow trough, or a decorative stone pool.

Cast-stone or concrete creatures make good fountains for children. They are whimsical garden pets, do the important work of recirculating water, and create a calming sound that permeates the whole backyard.

The beauty of this pond, built for the Pollack family of Leesburg, Virginia, lies in its restrained blend of counterbalancing design elements. The pond's smooth serenity is punctuated by tiny fountains and waterfalls.

A small pond is another relatively easy water feature for a child's garden. The simplest type has no pipes, pumps, or liner. Find a good spot (in the sun and out of the path of leaf-dropping trees), dig a hole twelve to twenty-four inches deep with sloping sides, and fill it with water. The larger the pond, the more interesting it will be to children. If the water seeps away too quickly, the pond can be lined with thick clay, a fiberglass shell, or flexible black rubber, which produces a deep, bottomless effect. Some families with very young children install a grid for safety. Children can splash, play with the bugs and frogs that inevitably come, race toy boats, conduct experiments, and fill watering cans to care for the rest of their garden.

meandering brooks

Real brooks twist and turn, wending their way around trees and rocks from their source, eventually finding their way to a larger stream, river, or lake. Simulated brooks are the same—except that their "source" is an electrically driven submersible pump, the same type used to recirculate water in outdoor fountains and many ponds. The pump forces water through a hose, buried in the ground or camouflaged by plants, to a high point and then lets gravity carry it back down its streambed pathway to a lower point or pool, where the perpetual cycle of circulation starts again. Although this description may sound less than romantic, the effects of a finely crafted brook can rival nature. The sound and sight of moving water will attract birds and other wildlife—including children.

A built stream in the wooded backyard of the Haden family of northern Virginia, designed by Kenneth S. Duffy, meanders eighty feet down the sloping site. The five children and their friends never tire of water games.

HOW A CHILD WISHES TO LIVE DOWN THERE!

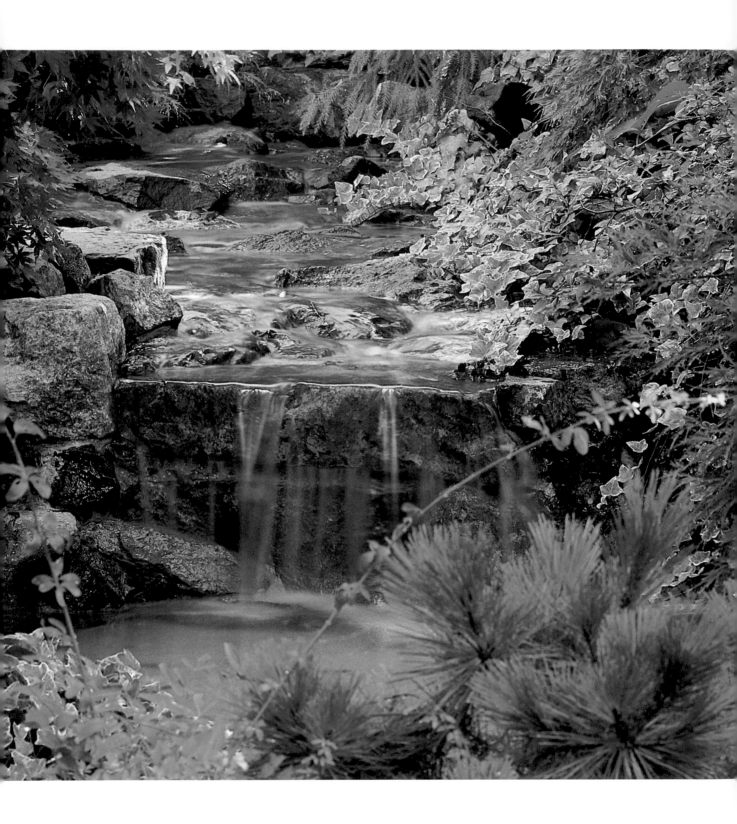

58   WE CAN SEE OUR COLOURED FACES FLOATING ON THE SHAKEN POOL

sensational waterfalls

Both the sound and the visual effects created by a waterfall are dramatic. Large ones create crashing sheets. Little ones make rushing spills. In a backyard recirculating stream and pond system, a waterfall can be formed anywhere in the path of the streambed—or at its end—by making an edge of flat stones and a drop-off of six inches to three feet or more. The farther the water drops, the more intense the sound. A small, accessible waterfall acts like a magnet on children, becoming a focal point for all their senses as it rushes over their hands or feet. It is also a highly appealing answer to the basic question posed by any recirculating system: how to get water from a high point to a low point.

Opposite: Constructed water-falls, like this one in the Shimizu family's garden in Glen Echo, Maryland, can be as mesmerizing as those produced by nature. Left: A small waterfall spills into a swirling pond in this backyard woodland created by Kibbe Turner in Bethesda, Maryland.

soothing pools

Built-in swimming pools—formal or naturalistic, made of concrete or rubber, edged with tile or stone— are so beckoning. And yet many parents of young children do not even consider them a backyard possibility. One obvious reason is expense; another is safety. For the Haden family of northern Virginia, whose five children and one large, deep swimming pool share the

backyard space, two further safety rules are in place. First, children are never allowed to enter the pool area unless an adult is present. Second, the pool area is protected by a motion-sensor security system; if anyone falls into the pool (or jumps in when an adult has not turned off the system), an alarm sounds. With these precautions established, the family's pool is a focal point for fun.

Above: To help children wade in safety, Isabelle Greene devised this "sandy beach" pool with a gently sloping, coarsely textured edge. Opposite: The Haden pool is fed by waterfalls that channel water from the baby pool, located above the wall at right.

JUST AS IF MOTHER HAD BLOWN OUT THE LIGHT!

creatures

In a world created by adult hands, run by adult clocks, and ordered by adult principles, children and animals are natural compatriots. Adults are often too busy with their tasks of planting, pruning, weeding, and mulching to notice the presence of butterflies, birds, and small mammals in the garden, but children adore backyard inhabitants, wild and domestic. Capitalize on their excitement by designing a garden that welcomes birds, bugs, bats, raccoons, opossums, and rabbits instead of considering them invaders. Creating an animal-friendly garden that exists in harmony with nature's systems—a garden that, as the environmentalist author Sara Stein says, "restores the ecology of our own backyards"—can be an exciting environmental adventure for children. Rightly done, it can take years, but there are some simple ways to get started. Libraries, cooperative extension agencies, state wildlife programs, and botanical gardens can provide information about local fauna and their habitats. And do not forget domestic animals. Outdoor houses and hutches for pets are often considered necessary evils to be hidden away in some out-of-sight corner of the yard. But a pet house can be one of the most interesting additions to the garden.

Animals add excitement to a child's garden. In this ecologically friendly garden, a baby fingernail-sized frog perches on a giant hosta leaf, creating an enchanted scene straight out of *Thumbelina*.

backyard habitats

Animals, like people, need food, water, cover, and places to mate and raise their young. Trees, shrubs, and other plants that produce nectar, nuts, berries, and seeds are a reliable source of food. For water, simply set out a basin, make a simple birdbath, scoop out a pond, or let rainwater collect in a barrel. For cover, provide a pile of brush, tree branches, or rocks or a hollow tree or log. And throw away all garden chemicals. To learn about local animals—what plants they eat and where they hide— take children for long walks around the neighborhood or local wildlife area. Add native plants to the garden to attract some of these, and soon children and adults will be coexisting with creatures once considered pests and predators.

The bat garden at George Washington's River Farm has everything that a small creature could want: varied plant materials for foraging, a pond for drinking, a cave for roosting, and a hollow log surrounded by a profusion of woody vines for hiding and nesting.

IN THAT FOREST TO AND FRO I CAN WANDER, I CAN GO;

f i s h   a n d   f r o g   p o n d s

Ruby red minnows dart beneath the surface of a small pond at River Farm, while frogs of all sizes populate the water and the rocky ledges of this water world.

A backyard pond can make a fine home for fish, frogs, and other amphibians if tended with a bit of environmental know-how. First, never use chemicals to keep the water free of algae. Instead, to oxygenate the water, plant the pond with water lilies, water hyacinth, water iris, duck potato, and sweet flag. Introduce black trap-door snails, which eat algae.

Leave out voracious large fish such as koi and carp, which eat the frog eggs and tadpoles that grow up into mosquito-devouring frogs. Stick with small fish such as ruby red minnows, shabunkins, and comets, add tadpoles in the spring, welcome the frogs that love to snack on pesky insects, and wait to see what other wild creatures come to congregate at the water's edge.

The best bird gardens have natural bird feeders—trees, shrubs, vines, flowers, and grasses that produce lots of berries, seeds, and nuts. Aim for variety. Good trees for cover include fir, juniper, spruce, pine, eastern red cedar, maple, and oak. For fruit, birds flock to serviceberry, hackberry, dogwood, hawthorn, crabapple, mulberry, cherry, and mountain ash trees. Fruit-producing shrubs include winterberry holly, elderberry, blueberry, viburnum, spicebush, yew, and brambles, such as blackberry. Flowers such as coreopsis, jack-in-the-pulpit, hollyhock, sunflower, poppy, larkspur, aster, and goldenrod provide seeds throughout the late summer and fall. And wild or ornamental grasses such as June grass, Indian grass, bluestem, and buffalo grass will provide seeds into the winter. Plantings should reflect natural patterns of differing heights and thicknesses to give birds privacy and room to move, hide, and preen. A hollow tree, rotting branch, or cluster of mature woody vines makes a good place to nest, as do hollow boxes hung in private, covered areas of the garden. Remember to provide year-round access to water for bathing as well as drinking.

Opposite: A diverse array of plants that offer tasty berries and seeds lures neighborhood birds into the Michaud family garden in Scituate, Massachusetts. A simple, child-height birdbath made of cast concrete offers them a place to splash and drink. Left: From a path flanked with blanket flower, Russian sage, and trumpet vine (a hummingbird favorite), Jane Hogue's tree-trunk bird hotel in Iowa arises in the distance. A shallow birdbath completes the fine-feathered accommodations.

butterfly ballets

Watching the interplay of butterflies and flowers, all of them different shapes, textures, and colors, is like viewing a tiny ballet. Children will spend hours spying on and chasing these whispery-winged visitors in a garden whose flowers are chosen specifically to lure them in. Butterflies are attracted to sweetly scented flowers in hues of purple, blue, orange, yellow, white, pink, and red. Butterflies also need sun, water, and shelter from heavy winds. For nectar, butterflies flock to buddleia, Joe Pye weed, purple coneflower, lantana, hyssop, columbine, red valerian, rabbit brush, tickseed, sedum, balsam, verbena, zinnia, yarrow, honeysuckle, and wisteria. Good host plants where those voracious caterpillars—the butterfly larvae—can eat to their heart's content include passion flower, Dutchman's pipe, parsley, milkweed, borage, fennel, and dill.

Butterflies abound in the lush Blue Ridge valley farmhouse garden that Sheela Lampietti designed while raising her four children. Purple coneflower, native to Virginia, is a magnet for attracting beautiful butterflies such as this swallowtail.

AND ABOVE THE DAISY TREE THROUGH THE GRASSES,

bountiful bats and bees

A standing hollow tree makes a good roosting spot for bats. This one was found in the woods and given a new home—the bat garden at River Farm. Bees, valuable garden visitors as well, enjoy the lavender, lobelia, and buddleia planted close by.

Children as well as adults often view bats and bees as less than desirable garden visitors. Bees might sting, and bats might bite. So the next logical thought is to avoid attracting them in any way. But clever parents may choose to do just the opposite: planting to attract these maligned creatures and teaching children caution as well as respect. Bees are important garden pollinators. Flowers that are especially enticing to them

include bee balm, mint, obedient plant, cosmos, blue lobelia, and lavender. North American bats, more akin to primates than rodents, keep to themselves during the day but help homeowners by devouring between two and three thousand insects every night. They also provide nitrogen-rich droppings (guano) to fertilize the garden. White, night-blooming flowers attract the moths and insects that bats love to eat.

p e t   p l a c e s

Why shouldn't a pet house be as
artistically designed as any other
decorative garden element? Pet
places are especially delightful
to children, who often crawl
inside and on top of them and
even imagine spending the night.
Families can make their own
fanciful dog, rabbit, cat, or guinea
pig houses, or they can look to
architects or designers for help.
The San Francisco landscape
architect Topher Delaney designs
avant-garde pet houses, including
a bounding bronze bunny rabbit
hutch and a galvanized metal
doghouse. Jack Rogers, an artisan
in Bolton, Massachusetts, makes
an insulated cedar doghouse with
a concave copper roof. Good
design need not be reserved for
humans—even the cat might like
a garden path made just for her.

**Right: Both children and their
bunnies enjoy this redwood
rabbit hutch. Opposite: Family
cats have right-of-way when
making tracks for the catnip
patch in one of Jane Hogue's
theme gardens in Iowa.**

LITTLE THINGS WITH LOVELY EYES SEE ME SAILING WITH SURPRISE.

refuges

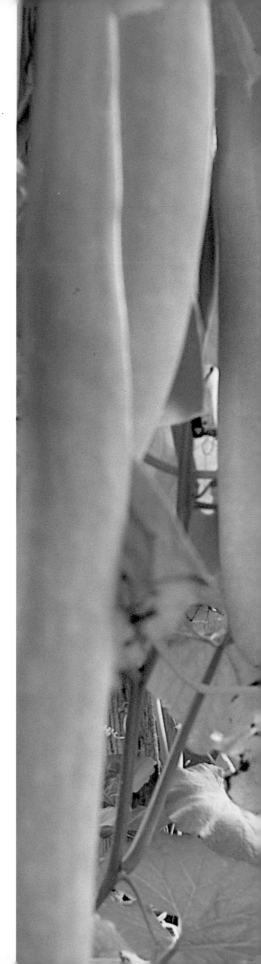

Children love enclosed, nestlike spaces, especially when they can see out but remain hidden. Researchers believe that this childhood tendency stems from an early survival instinct to seek unobtrusive places in which to hide from predators, with easy escape access and unblocked, long-range views. But enclosed spaces whose views and escape routes are cut off can quickly turn into dens of horror instead of cozy nests. A child who becomes trapped in an enclosed place with no visual sight lines—a closet whose door gets locked by a sibling or a large box whose flaps are closed down by a playmate—can become panic-stricken in seconds. Small spaces evoke both comfort and fear in children. Through imaginative play they enjoy poking around the edges of terror. Childhood stories involving mysterious forests (refuges with prospect) and menacing figures such as witches and big bad wolves (predators) enthrall each new generation. Games such as hide-and-seek never go out of style because of the excitement of hunting, being hunted, and finding spots to be safe. Plants and outdoor architecture can be used to create the dens, bowers, and caves children always seek.

By summer's end an ordinary garden arbor at Longwood Gardens, guarded by a terrifying scarecrow, is transformed into a mysterious enclosure dangling with gourds of all shapes and sizes.

bush and tree hideaways

Bushes and trees that can be hidden behind and inside are very important to children. One mother, after removing the old, overgrown foundation hedges from her yard, discovered, too late, that she had obliterated her children's favorite "hiding fort." When creating natural hideaways, choose (or at least do not remove) shrubs with soft, flexible leaves and branches— Japanese beautyberry, fraser and Japanese photinias, fringe tree, and black-haw and double-file viburnum—rather than thorny pyracanthas, pointy hollies, and prickly junipers. Camperdown elm and weeping varieties of mulberry, fig, willow, and beech all create umbrella-like canopies for hiding inside, while the Indian bean tree is a low, spreading tree with long, leathery seed pods. Groupings of feathery-needled cedar, hemlock, pine, yew, and arborvitae can create woodland enclosures into which a child will naturally nestle.

Right: At George Washington's River Farm, a tiny grove offers refuge amid pines, grasses, and perennials. Opposite, top and bottom: A weeping mulberry tree invites children to hide underneath its boughs.

TILL THE SHINING SCYTHES WENT FAR AND WIDE AND CUT IT DOWN TO DRY. **75**

v e g e t a b l e   b o w e r s

Beanpole tepees are a staple in the realm of children's garden ideas. They can be made easily of bamboo or any other strong, thin wood, tied at the top, and surrounded with seeds of quick-growing, vining vegetables. Beans such as scarlet runner and purple hyacinth mature fast, and their flowers are unexpectedly beautiful. Vegetable caves, tunnels, and arbors can be created using easy-to-bend willow or kousa dogwood or, for more permanent structures, steel electrical conduit tubing. Any vining vegetable, including squash, cucumbers, gourds, and baby pumpkins, is good for creating an enclosed space into which a child can crawl. At the peak of the season the child can climb inside her private bower and be greeted by a jubilant dangle of colorful, voluptuous vegetable life.

Bean vines quickly cover a garden tepee to create a vegetable playhouse for children. In building one, leave a doorway so that a child can enter without squeezing to fit or stomping on the crop. A cool floor of wood mulch is a finishing touch.

THESE GREEN AND SWEETLY SMELLING CROPS THEY LED IN WAGONS HOME;

Left: Enormous Chinese cucumbers dangle from a garden arbor in the Family Garden at the New York Botanical Garden. Above: Purple hyacinth bean is a vigorous climber. In just one season, it created this "kindergarten cave" at the Brooklyn Botanic Garden.

arbor retreats

A garden arbor is nothing more than a simple arch overgrown with plant materials. It can be made of bent twig, wood lattice, weatherproof resin, enameled steel, even trained living trees. Yet for all its simplicity an arbor can be one of the loveliest, coziest elements in any family garden. Small arbors with seats, placed against a brick wall or a wood fence, offer snug little sanctuaries for children, while arbors erected as arches along a pathway serve as gateways to other realms. Arbors should be tall enough for adults to pass through with ease. A child's refuge need not actually be inaccessible to parents, but it should feel that way in a child's imagination.

The organic gardener Shepherd Ogden erected this arbor as a gateway into his children's playhouse garden in Londonderry, Vermont. The arbor, made of simple wood lattice, was quickly covered in one season by a profusion of climbing vines.

O WHAT A JOY TO CLAMBER THERE,

miniature forests

In enclosed yards, even small ones, a miniature woodland area will serve children's needs nearly as well as the real thing. An area as small as two feet by eight feet is the minimum space required. Fast-growing, tall, thin bamboo is a natural choice for a small forest, but beware: bamboo is extremely invasive and must be carefully managed. Another, much slower route is to use a number of tree types with varying growth habits and height ranges and to intersperse a multitude of low-growing ground covers. Being inside a forest is fun for children only if they have a clear-cut way out, so be sure to include a curving path, covered with wood mulch, pine needles, leaves, or pebbles.

This grove of palm and bamboo in the Jungles-Yates garden, Coconut Grove, Florida, is tiny—only about eight feet in diameter—but it feels like a secluded forest to the children who play in it every day, Amanda and Benjamin Jungles.

WITH THE SWEET, THE DIM, THE DUSTY AIR,

w i l l o w   n e s t s

The ancient tradition of willow weaving, more familiar in Europe than in the United States, can be used to create charming, rustic garden arches, tunnels, arbors, caves, and walls. Willow or other fast-growing, pliable, durable woods such as red osier dogwood and hazel are good for producing living and nonliving garden sculpture. For a nonliving arch, divide the shoots into two groups and bend together the tops to create an arch; then fasten the tops with twine. Loosely weave the legs and then stabilize them in the ground. For a living arch, plant individual cuttings in the ground and weave their tops to create individual arches. Planting a little thicket of willow along the back edge of the yard ensures a steady supply of new shoots for experimentation.

Willow is used worldwide. Opposite, clockwise from top left: a nest poetically named "Huddle Up," Yorkshire Sculpture Park, England; a living willow dome, Ryton Organic Gardens, England; a snowy nest, Clapham, England; a sinuous snake, Brasov, Romania. Left: A living willow tunnel, created for the Tsurugi Art Festival, Japan.

woodland cottages

A tiny outdoor house is an enchanting object for a child. Too small for adults to enter and distanced from a child's real house, it offers kids the imaginative possibility of being in a land far, far away from the adult world. A playhouse need not be elaborate to meet a child's needs, although architect-designed models from Gothic to contemporary are available. A child will play just as happily in a simple hut, such as the Little House on the Prairie at George Washington's River Farm in Alexandria, Virginia, whose charm derives as much from surrounding plant materials—a lush blend of wildflowers and prairie grasses—as from its simple, rustic structure.

Right: Situating this fenced-in, double-decker playhouse on the edge of a woods creates a sense of mystery in the Michaud family garden in Scituate, Massachusetts. Opposite: Geometric cutouts for windows and doors add whimsy to a postmodern cottage in Bethesda, Maryland.

WHAT ARE YOU ABLE TO BUILD WITH YOUR BLOCKS?

CASTLES AND PALACES, TEMPLES AND DOCKS.

Above: Framed by climbing pole beans, Molly and Sam Ogden peep out the window of their garden playhouse in Londonderry, Vermont. Right: The Little House on the Prairie, created at George Washington's River Farm, is surrounded by a profusion of low-maintenance prairie grasses and wildflowers.

RAIN MAY KEEP RAINING, AND OTHERS GO ROAM,

BUT I CAN BE HAPPY AND BUILDING AT HOME.

dirt

Whether parents like it or not, kids love to play in the dirt. They delight in digging swales through it, building mounds, constructing earth tunnels, castles, and caves. My mother spent summers playing with nothing more than three matchbox cars, building an entire world for them out of found objects. She and a friend constructed roads, tunnels, bridges, filling stations, neighborhoods, and carports out of earth, tree roots, sticks, and stones. In a time of no television and few possessions, she stayed outside all day long playing in a world made entirely from nature. Such open ended "loose parts" play, say researchers, is far superior for children's minds and bodies than play limited by prefabricated or predetermined elements; inventiveness in any environment is inspired by the variables found there. Children need the opportunity to be architects and builders themselves, and they need access to the raw materials to carry out this essential imaginative work. The importance of sand play for children is well documented. According to the theory of loose parts, play with dirt, sticks, and stones falls into the same realm. Children's gardens must accommodate this messy need to dig, mold, build up, and tear down.

Getting their hands grimy is natural for children. Parents should make space in the family garden for the dirty work of childhood—poking, prodding, digging, building, and burying.

earth berms

Children like variation in scale in their play landscapes. Any adult who ever played outdoors as a child has some memory of finding a giant hill of mounded sand, dirt, or mulch and spending a morning or an afternoon simply running up and down this miniature mountain. Earth berms and mounds in the backyard can be more than temporary joys resulting from some type of excavation. They can serve as deliberate, permanent creations and, for longer wear, can be covered with grass. When the residents of Marion Park on Capitol Hill in Washington, D.C., reconfigured their neighborhood public playground, they retained the four well-loved earth mounds as a surround for a new children's play area. These are as well used as the prefabricated climbing equipment. In addition to topological interest, the variation in grade creates more secluded areas for play.

At the Brooklyn Botanic Garden's Children's Discovery Garden, an array of tiny, grassy earth berms, each no more than two feet high, makes the toddlers' play area a place of delight.

Offer children a small trowel or even a kitchen spoon and a spot where excavation is acceptable—next to a vegetable patch or playhouse, for example—and watch their imaginations flower.

What to do about the need to dig? Designate an area of the garden for this purpose. Children need situations where the elements of play are not predetermined. But parents appreciate beauty and order. One way to camouflage children's digging pits from "presentable" outdoor space is to erect a wall of interesting plant materials, such as tall, tough feather reed grass, or a woven wall of willow or hazel saplings

to screen the area from direct adult view. At the Coombs School in Berkshire, England, a permanent clay pit was created in a secluded section of the grounds. Occasionally the children make sculpture from the clay. Fables about worlds existing beneath the earth's surface are part of almost every culture. Letting children physically explore such imaginative possibilities lets them flex their minds as well as their muscles.

FAR IN THE PLOTS, I SEEM HIM DIG, OLD AND SERIOUS, BROWN AND BIG.

simple sandboxes

One simple way to allow for children's play with loose parts is to provide an area designated for sand. Children like sand because of its magical tactility. Adults like it because it is inexpensive and keeps children occupied for hours. Sandboxes made of wood or other natural materials coexist easily with children's gardens. Unfortunately, most sandboxes that can be purchased are unattractive as well as blatantly intrusive on the land-scape. Large green plastic turtles with hollow bodies and removable plastic lids are so ubiquitous that most parents do not even realize that there are other, more artful alternatives: large-scale "sandscapes," which can be created by giving over extensive areas of the yard to sand and sometimes stone; unobtrusive "sand valleys" surrounded by earth and plant materials; and naturalistic "sand beaches."

A seven-by-ten-foot sandlot, nestled into a palm-shaded clearing, blends seamlessly with its tropical backyard landscape in the Jungles-Yates garden, Coconut Grove, Florida. The sand is replen-ished every six months or so.

TO DIG THE SANDY SHORE.

MY HOLES WERE EMPTY LIKE A CUP, IN EVERY HOLE THE SEA CAME UP,

Opposite: With a built stream on one side and benches on the other, this Bethesda, Maryland, sandlot attracts the whole family. Left: A sandbox can be elegant yet easy to create: little more than a cutaway area in a terrace or walkway. Above: A simple square with an unobtrusive acrylic lid, created by Oehme, van Sweden and Associates, is tucked into a brick patio.

Dirt can be more than a sculpting medium for children. It can also be a place where abundant treasures—small, shiny, or interestingly textured articles— are waiting to be excavated. Playground dirt is often full of bottle caps, broken glass, concrete rubble, hair barrettes, animal bones, gum wrappers, and tiny electronic components. But at the Brooklyn Botanic Garden's new Children's Discovery Garden, children are encouraged to collect and play with "nature's toys"— pine cones, berries, seeds, pods, twigs, leaves, and stems. And unlike at most other public gardens, children are allowed to take their treasures home with them. Parents can follow this garden's lead by letting natural treasures accumulate in their own yard for children to discover.

In the Children's Discovery Garden at the Brooklyn Botanic Garden, natural treasures are not overlooked. Children may raid containers of pine cones, sticks, and stones and play with them in whichever way they like.

s t i c k s   a n d   s t o n e s

Parents generally do not want their children to play with sticks and stones because they are so easily—and readily—used as weapons. Busy parents often forbid dangerous things because they do not have the time or energy to teach children how to use them wisely and creatively. But sticks and stones can have a place in a child's garden. Parents and children can collect them together, making piles in various areas of the yard to be raided as needed for continuing imaginative work and play. Encourage children's openness to architectural experimentation by letting them use sticks and stones to make simple buildings and sculpture. Before long, they will be immersed in their own fantastical creative projects.

Children love to discover and create. Objects from nature offer more diversity in shape, texture, and visual appeal than any collection of store-bought toys. Out of sticks and stones can arise mountains and cities.

h e i g h t s

In ancient times, castles and fortresses were situated on hills and people believed that gods resided on mountaintops. Today tourists tromp in droves to the elevators that zip them to the top of the Empire State Building—seeking high ground is a natural human impulse. For children, climbing is one of the most alluring of all activities. As soon as they develop the ability to toddle around, they begin gravitating toward high places. But as universally attempted as it is, unregulated climbing seems to be one of the most universally condemned activities a child can choose to pursue. Although backyards and play parks are filled with prefabricated climbing structures, children are told that tree climbing, fence scaling, and other self-directed adventures involving heights are too dangerous. Of course children can hurt themselves, and they must be respectful of property. But parents should offer children more freedom when their climbing does not seem to be detrimental to themselves or anyone else. They should also look beyond store-bought climbing structures as the only acceptable way of addressing children's need to climb. A child-friendly garden can have other artistic, adventurous, natural ways to accommodate climbing.

Children naturally seek high territory, where they can survey the earth as well as the sky. The branches of a hundred-year-old weeping beech at the Brooklyn Botanic Garden make it a king among climbers—and carvers.

trees for climbing

Not every yard comes equipped with mature climbing trees, but growing a few is not an impossible task. Trees for climbing should spread horizontally, with branches that start low enough to the ground for a child to get a leg up without having to shimmy up the trunk (maples are good, poplars are not). A climbing tree should be a hardwood; softwood trees are easily damaged, and their branches are thin, weak, and dangerous. Some of the fastest-growing hardwood trees (ready to climb within five to seven years) include Norway and silver maple, pin and willow oak, American sycamore and its cousin the London plane tree, Chinese chestnut, Chinese elm, and the universally beloved tree of childhood, the weeping willow. Apple, mulberry, and many other fruit trees are also good choices. The catalpa is a great climber, with giant elephant-ear leaves and strange seed pods that look like green beans. Or plant slow-growing hickory or beech as a legacy for babies yet to be born.

Right: Mulberries have great branches. Opposite, clockwise from top left: Perfect climbers— apple (with climbing roses), oak, Norway maple, and willow.

WHO SHOULD CLIMB BUT LITTLE ME?

bewitching tree houses

A tree house offers so many of the elements that children seek in their play—refuge, height, and physical challenge. Tree houses do not have to be extremely high to feel adventurous to a child, nor do they require a mature tree. For the Children's Garden at Red Butte Garden in Salt Lake City, the Colorado landscape architect Herb Schaal of EDAW designed a "growing tree house"—a playhouse on stilts five feet off the ground, under which he planted a staghorn sumac. The fast-growing tree's branches will grow up and around the little house in just two seasons—"a nearly instant tree house," says Schaal. Tree houses can be dangerous if they are poorly constructed, however. All states have codes regarding structures built off the ground, so be aware of local restrictions before beginning any tree house project.

Sinuous branches create a tree house that looks as if it sprouted of its own accord. Safe, sturdy, and playfully rendered, this rustic design in Cave Junction, Oregon, allows kids to pretend that they are in an untamed space.

Left: Although natural materials are preferable, colorful plastic pipes are sturdy and can be constructed and dismantled quickly. Above: A whole tree is not required for a tree house. This nautical example on Bainbridge Island, Washington, is perched on an enormous maple stump. A staircase hollowed out of the center allows pirates and their friends to set sail securely.

natural play structures

Most adults remember the metal monkey bars at school as a major place to "hang," and most also remember broken teeth, broken bones, or hurt backs incurred by falling onto the hard concrete or asphalt. Today playgrounds are required to have softer surfaces that lessen the impact of falls, but more than a few children still hurt themselves. Prefabricated climbing sets have their place. Most children love them. But they are not the only way to accommodate children's climbing behavior. (Nor will any one method prevent all accidents.) Good alternatives are natural climbing structures—large boulders, vines, stalks, bent trunks, low limbs, and even downed trees—all of which allow for the joy of physical challenge without marring the backyard landscape with unnecessarily complicated devices.

Logs and boulders make excellent balance beams and obstacle courses. The Brooklyn Botanic Garden's Discovery Garden draws together these natural materials for climbing, jumping, and acrobatic feats.

magical beanstalks

As children know, "Jack and the Beanstalk" is a tale about the treasures and dangers that await a boy who leaves solid ground for cloudy territory via a magic beanstalk that reaches into the sky after just one night's growth. The Michigan 4-H Children's Garden at Michigan State University in East Lansing offers an imaginative way of presenting this story by using a tall wooden pole, a set of waterproof paints, and a package of fast-growing bean seeds, such as scarlet runner or purple hyacinth. Magical decorations can be painted over the pole and left to dry. (A coating of polyurethane will protect the wood even further.) The pole should be stabilized in the ground and the beans planted in a circle around the pole. Before long the "beanstalk" will be covered with lush foliage and brightly colored flowers and pods. Another version is a tall, stripped sunflower stalk, perfect for climbing.

When children are involved, the most unanticipated transformations take place in the garden. A giant sunflower, stripped of its leaves and with its top supported by a clothesline, can become a magic beanstalk leading up to the clouds.

m o v e m e n t

Weary parents often feel as if they are in a time warp: their children's speed of movement, powered by seemingly superhuman energy, can seem ten times that of their own. Medical studies show that this is nearly the case. A child's brain has pleasure centers that are highly sensitive to the stimulation of rapid movement. This is why children are so happy when they are twirling in an endless circle, swinging as high as they can go, or jumping from the deck to the patio a hundred times in a row, laughing hysterically all the while; their bodies are being flooded with endorphins. A harmonious family garden is one where neither the adults' nor the children's desires obliterate the other's. Swings and slides give children the chance to satisfy this need for body movement, as do riding tricycles, shooting basketballs, and jumping on trampolines. But backyard mechanisms for movement do not have to blight the landscape. Swings, slides, wagon paths, jumping areas, and basketball court designs can be aesthetically appealing, subtle and organic instead of shamelessly amusement-park-like, while offering children every opportunity to experience the intoxicating bodily engagement they crave.

Children need room to run, play, twirl, and somersault. A soft grassy or mulched area, such as the one incorporated into the Michaud family's garden in Scituate, Massachusetts, is essential for active games.

indispensable lawns

The wide, water-guzzling, chemically weed-free, constantly mown American lawn is ecologically incorrect. For at least a decade American gardeners have been chided to eliminate their lawns or at least to replace a part of them with ecologically mindful xeriscapes—landscapes designed to grow and thrive with only rainwater. But maintaining a mown area large enough for children to play on is extremely useful. As an arena for children's games, sports, and acrobatics, there is no substitute for a soft, grassy lawn, artfully placed, as one element in a family's outdoor living space. The lawn need not dominate the garden, nor must it be flat. Demon water guzzlers though lawns may be, Americans became obsessed with them for a reason: lawns are sweet and embracing, soft and safe, perfect pads for rest and recreation.

A verdant playing lawn in Florence, South Carolina, is bordered by a billowing edge of landscaped woodland and dotted with brass croquet hoops in the shapes of the children's favorite animals.

WILLIE COCKS HIS HIGHLAND BONNET, JOHNNIE BEATS THE DRUM.

soaring swings

A swing is one of childhood's great delights. Many parents remember two types of swings from their own childhoods. One, dutifully erected in the backyard, was probably some variant of the standard aluminum model. But the other type of swing—the wild version—was found in some undeveloped neighborhood lot, erected by some unknown band of children at some unknown time in the past. The appeal of such untamed swings, along with rope ladders leading to tree forts and Tarzan vines reaching across excavated craters, is that they simultaneously facilitate both movement and imagination. To feed children's capacity for enrapturing physical experiences that extend beyond the realm of mere exercise, parents should for-go the aluminum equipment and go for simplicity or natural materi-als. Try hanging a swing from a sturdy tree branch and watch your child's imagination soar.

So ubiquitous are heavy-duty, canvas-seated, steel-chained swings attached to factory-made aluminum or steel frames and set in concrete that many of us have forgotten that a child's swing can actually be a thing of beauty.

FEET IN TIME, ALERT AND HEARTY,

Swooshing down a slide is the outdoor equivalent of eating potato chips—it is almost impossible to stop. Once children get moving on a slide, the pattern is predictable: they run to the ladder, climb up as fast as possible, position themselves at the apex, push forward, glide down to the ground, and start the cycle all over. Slides enhance all types of running and catching games and become more intriguing with organic designs— a circular slide that twists around a tree, a secret shoot that emerges from the shadows of a tiny deck, a slide that extends from a house on stilts, surrounded by mysterious tall grasses. Families can look to creative play equipment manufacturers and landscape designers to help them custom design an imaginative, stylish, action-packed slide that blends beautifully into their own backyard.

A child's sliding board can be a garden centerpiece. In this southern California backyard, a fanciful tower with a zippy yellow slide is surrounded by walls of Texas privet laid out in a simple, formal English style.

b a l l t r i c k s

That a basketball hoop and paved half-court can be part of an artful garden plan may seem unbelievable, but some designs have incorporated basketball play well. In a garden in Chevy Chase, Maryland, the landscape architect Nancy Denig persuaded the owner not to cover a large area in the back with concrete. Instead the "court" is made of bluestone and serves double duty as a wide pad that connects the front and sides of the house. The playing area is almost completely camouflaged from the street by tall feather reed grass, which is rugged enough to withstand the pummeling of errant balls. The Miami landscape architect Raymond Jungles ensured that his children's basketball hoop is nearly invisible in the garden: its backstop is made of Plexiglas, and its pole and hoop are painted dark green.

With its clear backstop, the Jungles-Yates basketball hoop fades into the foliage of the orchid and palm trees in their Coconut Grove, Florida, garden. The concrete brick basketball court serves double duty as a pleasant patio for fans.

jumping jacks and jills

Children love to jump on beds.
When they get a little older, many
love the high-flying pleasure of
jumping on a trampoline. For
parents who want to indulge their
children's appetite for jumping in
the out-of-doors but do not have the
room or desire for a trampoline,
other captivating alternatives exist.
One lovely way to turn children's
proclivity for jumping into a
musical, mathematical dance is to
build into the garden pavement a
set of German dance chimes. Each
of the nine large square bronze
"keys" of the dance chimes peals
out a different bell-toned note when
a child jumps on it. Children learn
to use their feet to play a musical
instrument, and everyone enjoys a
magical garden element.

**Children love jumping, pushing
buttons, and making music.
A set of in-ground dance chimes
at the Michigan 4-H Children's
Garden allows them to do all
these at once. Each bronze "key"
peals out a rich bell-toned note
as children learn musical
improvization with their feet.**

circular courses

Why do children chase one another around the kitchen table a hundred times a night? Why do they run in endless circles around the backyard picnic table? Running in a circle seems comforting, allowing a child to keep moving without leaving familiar territory. It is also mesmerizing: because the child does not have to decide where his next step should be, his body can simply enjoy undistracted continuous movement. Creating a circular pathway in the backyard will give children season after season of pleasurable perpetual motion. An extremely wide pathway allows room for unruly wagons and side-by-side skating. The renowned landscape designer Thomas Church noted that "a circular route in the garden can provide more amusement hours for small children than any number of swings or slides."

A wide circular pathway adds both beauty and utility to a yard, offering children a never-ending course for running, skating, tricycling, or pulling wagons. This flagstone and brick path at St. Mark's Episcopal Church, Washington, D.C., is used for myriad chasing games.

NOW THAT WE'VE BEEN ROUND THE VILLAGE, LET'S GO HOME AGAIN.

make-believe

Children in any kind of environment make up imaginary worlds. City children build forts and dens out of old bed springs and abandoned chairs. Suburban children mold their environment with objects from the house, schoolyard, and neighborhood. But botanically complex backyards specifically designed to enhance imaginative play can open doors into worlds children might never have entered. There are a few archetypal physical experiences no child should grow up without. A child can read a book in which a heroine travels down a secret path in the woods, or she can walk down a mysterious overgrown path herself. A child can watch a television program in which the hero gets lost in a mazelike trap, or he can experience the challenge of unpuzzling a real maze himself. As the pioneering early childhood educator Maria Montessori stressed, nothing—except of course a wise teacher—is more important in a child's early education than a "prepared environment." An adult's job is to prepare the environment; a child's job is to discover its mysteries. The challenge for parents is to pepper the backyard with enough surprises that children will always be happening on some new delight that awakens a new part of their consciousness.

The Story Garden in Portland, Oregon, a low-level maze of grass and cobblestones, offers stories told in etched granite pavement along its pathways.

WHEN CHILDREN ARE PLAYING ALONE ON THE GREEN,

s e c r e t   p a t h s

Plain walkways that lead matter-of-factly to a fountain or flower bed are not very appealing to children's imaginations. A naturalistic path, however, leads to something unseen, hidden by flowers, foliage, branches, or architecture—and thus is totally open to imaginative speculation. The path's pavement design can also be of great interest to children. Parents can imprint leaves, flower petals, a cat's paws, or children's hands and feet in concrete stepping stones. Use colored concrete to make a yellow brick road. Mortar together varying sizes of pebbles, recycled glass, glittery rocks, and bits of wood to make a crazy-quilt path. Grow Irish moss, creeping mint, or lemon thyme between the cracks. Children will love living with a path full of surprises that they can travel and discover for themselves.

Opposite, clockwise from top left: The garden path in a variety of materials—irregularly cut stone; colored concrete and black slate, a Delaney, Cochran and Castillo design; a curved swath of grass; and an enticing red brick road. Left: Rubble, pebbles, tough herbs, and ornamental grass create a whimsical footway.

Above and opposite: Designers of the Michigan 4-H Children's Garden worried that expansive stretches of concrete required to make the garden accessible to wheelchairs would be too stark. The solution? Hundreds of visiting children's handprints bring the concrete to life.

WHEN CHILDREN ARE HAPPY AND LONELY AND GOOD,

Left: This sunny herb-border path in a family garden combines the formality of square slate stepping stones, laid diagonally, with an informal rough-cut stone edge.

m e s m e r i z i n g   m a z e s

The maze is one of the most ancient impositions of human design on the landscape. Uncannily similar remnants of circular labyrinth designs have been found in the ruins of ancient cultures all around the globe. Today mazes of earth, turf, hedges, and stone repeat these ancient patterns. The experience of being inside a maze and trying to find a way out is different from tracing an exit from a maze printed on a page. And the experience of following a maze of stepping stones in the grass is different from walking in a maze of hedges, enclosed on all sides by leafy walls. Good evergreen shrubs for starting a hedge maze include privet, boxwood, arborvitae, and juniper. Young hedges form a border with seamless sides within two years if they are planted close together. Stone mazes can be created from rocks collected in the yard or neighborhood.

Right: Mazes made of tall, leafy hedges are not the only game in town. Swirling brick pathways set in grass can also offer children mesmerizing journeys, as demonstrated by Veronica's Maze in Parham Park, England.

HE LIES ON THE LAURELS, HE RUNS ON THE GRASS,

Above: The Champion family's front-yard "pocket maze" in northern California creates a three-dimensional experience out of stone walls and pathways, raised earth and wildflowers, all in eighteen by twenty-four feet.

Espaliered trees—ones whose branches are trained to grow in an ornamental design along a flat plane—are enchanting additions to children's gardens. First, because they look otherworldly, they can be an extremely compelling focus for a child's imagination. Second, because maintaining them requires continuous intervention by human hands, parents cannot help but be drawn into the garden with children on a regular basis. Dwarf fruit trees, dogwood, ornamental quince, and climbing euonymous are all good choices for espaliering. Branches can be trained to grow naturalistically, geometrically, or in whimsical shapes. If the idea is tempting but the execution seems daunting, trees that have already begun to be trained can be found at nurseries, along with full instructions on how to maintain them.

An apple tree's flexible branches make it a good choice for espaliering. This whimsical heart shape was created by splitting the trunk and training the branches with horizontal wires.

WHENE'ER YOU ARE HAPPY AND CANNOT TELL WHY,

Above left: This reindeer at Filoli in Woodside, California, is the fast kind of topiary, made by stuffing a sculptural form with sphagnum moss and planting it with ivy. Right: A trained and clipped variety of topiary is made from potted boxwood.

Growing a topiary shaped like an animal—a cat, a bear, a chicken, you name it—is a lovely way for children to cultivate a menagerie of shaggy green pets. These decorative shapes created of plant materials can be made either by trimming a dense shrub, such as boxwood, holly, hornbeam, or privet, or by constructing (or buying) an ornamental wood or metal frame and training ivy over it. When topiary is created using sculptural forms (the easier way to make topiary for families with young children), parents can teach children to gently train the ivy around the frame. As they do with their stuffed animals, children will pretend that their green outdoor animals are living creatures in need of nurture, and their nurturing proclivities can be well directed to an activity that is also fun.

t a l l   g r a s s e s

Standing in a field of tall grasses blowing in the wind is a mesmerizing experience. An imaginative child can wade through fields of soft grass as high as her chest and pretend to be Moses' sister Miriam, hiding in the bulrushes while keeping an eye on the baby in a reed basket. Kurt Bluemel, a highly regarded nurseryman who specializes in ornamental grasses, recommends Evergold sedge, Overdam reed grass, Elijah's Blue fescue, and wild oats as soft, feathery, not-too-frighteningly tall choices for children's gardens. The landscape architect Herb Schaal of EDAW suggests scattering prairie grass seed for a meadow-like effect and then mowing a curving path so that children will not be intimidated about wading through it—a small effort that makes grass less daunting.

Right: A waving sea of ornamental grasses in differing heights creates a sense of lush wildness in the landscape at the National Zoo in Washington, D.C. For the naturalistic Olmsted Walk here, Oehme, van Sweden and Associates combined giant Chinese silver grass and shorter oriental fountain grass for contrast.

Above: In the Enchanted Garden of the Michigan 4-H Children's Garden, tall, whispery Fairy's Joke grass, weighed down with tiny plantlets instead of seeds, is juxtaposed with soft Bunnies' Tail grass, which grows in the beds just beyond.

spectacular sunflowers

With its oversized face and bright yellow fringe, the sunflower towers over all other garden elements in its popularity among children. Scores of sunflower varieties are available in every height, blossom size, and hue. A sunflower garden can be created by mixing three to five distinctly different varieties. For a sunflower playhouse, intersperse morning glory seeds between two rows of sunflower seeds, spaced playhouse distance apart (about five or six feet). As they grow, train the morning glory vines around the sunflower stems. As the summer progresses, the morning glories will quickly climb to the sunflower's blooms. To create a "roof," wind twine back and forth across the sunflower heads to make an archway frame for the morning glories to vine around and create a canopy of shade.

This sunflower house is one of the many theme gardens that Jane Hogue designed for her children on the family's farm in Odebolt, Iowa. Heavenly Blue morning glories planted in between the sunflowers can create garden walls and, by August, a shady roof.

WHEN AT HOME ALONE I SIT AND AM VERY TIRED OF IT,

Left: Giant Grey-Stripe sunflowers brighten a rustic hickory trellis. Above: A mass of Indian Blanket sunflowers entices a young gardener at the U.S. National Arboretum's Children's Garden in Washington, D.C.

a r t f u l   o r n a m e n t

The best garden adornments are living ones, but child-friendly artworks of wood, metal, and stone are also fun. At the Orleans Infant School in Twickenham, England, the children drew pictures of people or animals that they would like to have as sculpture in their schoolyard. From these drawings an artist-in-residence created life-sized wooden garden dwellers that were perched and hung throughout the yard. "Magic mirrors," with brightly painted frames, can be easily made and popped into planting beds. Sculpture that personifies nature and creature sculptures, made from household caulk and placed on tree trunks, are other good examples. With whimsy as the guiding principle, adults and children are bound to come up with great ideas.

Right top: A wooden beast with wings plays his trumpet for students at the Orleans Infant School in England. Bottom: A magic mirror enlivens an herb bed at St. Werberg's Park Nursery School in Bristol, England. Opposite: The "North Wind" sculpture at Brookside Gardens, Wheaton, Maryland, blows across the Pollinators Garden to entertain visitors.

TO THE FAIRY LAND AFAR WHERE THE LITTLE PEOPLE ARE....

For a child a garden gate can be a door to new worlds. It does not have to lead anywhere or even be part of a fence. Its primary attraction is that it is attached to hinges, can be opened and closed, and can be run through again and again. A child's gate should be simple to maneuver, with an easy latching system. For even more appeal it can be adorned with engraved or welded images from nature or nursery stories. Built-in archways can be overgrown each year with a different whimsical annual vine, such as luffa gourd or purple hyacinth bean. Position the gate to open onto a special area of the yard— a wooded spot or a cultivated herb and vegetable area— as if opening onto a new world.

A garden gate can be made magical in many simple ways. Oversized pumpkin leaves and vines cover this gate with lush mystery. A spooky sculpted mask hung on the pickets adds even more fantasy to the garden.

f a n c i f u l   f e n c e s

If a new fence is out of the question, an old one can be made child-friendly with paint, ornament, the addition of a climbing vine, like this Virginia creeper, or even a peephole at just the right height for a kid.

A fence is one of the most conspicuous of garden components. Because it may be the first thing one notices, it can define the character of the garden. But fences are often selected quickly and erected haphazardly when they should be chosen deliberately and built carefully. Erecting a fence is an opportunity for a family to learn together—about stone masonry techniques rarely used today, for example. Throughout Europe, walls

of domestic gardens are commonly made of stone—tiny pebbles, bricks interspersed with stones, dry-laid walls. Fences made of unmilled wood or fanciful pickets are also charming. Even wire mesh supported by wood posts, if camouflaged with honeysuckle, shrubs, or vines, can evoke a sense of country wildness. Select a fence design that blends well with and enhances the garden's style, and then make it unique.

playful peepholes

Poking out knotholes in fences or finding empty spaces to peep through has always been a favorite way for children to feel that they know secrets hidden on the other side. Peepholes can be planned as part of a fence or gate design from the start. At the Michigan 4-H Children's Garden in East Lansing, the four-foot-tall brick fence surrounding the Secret Garden has peepholes situated two-and-one-half feet high all the way around it. Holes can be drilled easily in wood fences and accentuated with playful designs painted in waterproof paint. Even hedge fences and mazes can have peepholes. The landscape architect Herb Schaal of EDAW suggests creating metal cutouts in geometric and animal shapes and interspersing them between young boxwood, juniper, arborvitae, or privet hedges. The shrubs will grow around the forms, creating leaf-enclosed peepholes.

Children do not have to stand on tiptoe to peek into the Secret Garden at the Michigan 4-H Children's Garden. Child-height, brick-sized peepholes were strategically placed around the garden's curving brick wall.

WHEN MY EYES I ONCE AGAIN OPEN, AND SEE ALL THINGS PLAIN; . . .

lilliputian furniture

Furniture that is just the right size is special for a child. Big chairs make little feet dangle. Big tables come up to children's chins. Small furniture gives children a bit more control in a world whose scale already keeps many things beyond their reach. But finding beautifully designed garden furniture in miniature is not easy. Small cast-aluminum cafe tables and chairs; English teak outdoor dining sets; miniature Adirondack chairs in painted wood; weatherproof mahogany rockers; and whimsically carved redwood benches—all are made by well-known garden furniture designers, but finding out that these tiny pieces even exist requires combing through catalogues or making special requests. Ask your local fine garden furniture dealer whether any of its manufacturers carries a children's line. You may be pleasantly surprised.

A tiny garden chair, made of weather-resistant redwood, is hand carved with pictures of woodland animals by Reed Brothers artisans. Children adore having their very own furniture for special outdoor spots.

n u r t u r e

Most children enjoy caring tenderly for something other than themselves. They can translate to plants their experience as nurturers of dolls, pets, and one another if their parents provide a model for them to imitate. Parents can offer children of the tenderest ages a few containers on the deck or a small plot of ground in the yard and help them fill it with plants. Giving children a plot of their own can yield amazing results. Younger children will need more help selecting plant materials, watering, and weeding. But after a few years of steering, they might just take off on their own. By growing vegetables they get fast, tasty results and can try something new every year. By growing abundantly productive annual flowers they have the irresistible opportunity to pick with abandon. By growing herbs they learn that plants have a variety of useful purposes, from providing pleasant perfumes to spicing spaghetti. With berry bushes or fruit trees they gain a garden legacy that matures with them. Try starting the process by choosing plant materials from the examples that follow. Many of these are edible as well as beautiful.

Tyler Hogue surveys the theme gardens at his family's farm in Odebolt, Iowa. His own personal creation is a barnyard garden, filled with plants whose names incorporate those of farm animals—cockscomb, hen and chicks, goatsbeard, cowbells, pig weed, and toad flax.

136

Vegetable gardens have always been popular choices for children. Because they produce in one season and children quickly see the results of their labor, vegetables can be the way into the world of "growing their own." To make the experience all the more special, parents may want to present out-of-the-ordinary vegetables that have magical overtones. Some varieties come in tiny sizes, such as bird-egg-sized Bambino eggplant, Sugarbaby watermelon, and Tom Thumb lettuce. Other vegetables grow to giant proportions, including yard-long Chinese pole beans, three-foot Yamato cucumbers, and Big Max pumpkins, which can reach one hundred pounds. Oddly colored vegetables are another fun idea—yellow watermelons, blue potatoes, white tomatoes, Easter egg–colored radishes. Many colorful varieties exist. But even if the family decides to choose less eccentric selections, the real magic is in growing, harvesting, and eating food fresh from the earth.

Above: Chef Alice Waters, proprietor of the world-famous Chez Panisse restaurant in Berkeley, California, shares garden-fresh lettuce with her daughter, Fanny. Opposite, clockwise from top left: To a child, fresh-harvested broccoli could be a miniature tree. Radishes (top and bottom right) show children that wonderful things can be pulled from the dirt. Sam Ogden, the son of the organic gardener Shepherd Ogden, plants seeds in the Cook's Garden in Vermont.

AS AT EVE BEHIND THE PANE FROM MY EYES IT FAINTED.

Above: A backyard pumpkin patch is an easy way to make the harvest days of October all the more fun for kids. Right: The New York Botanical Garden's teaching gardens spill forth with amaranth, tomatoes, basil, squash, nasturtium, lettuce, and more delights that encourage children to eat what they grow.

JUST AS IT WAS SHUT AWAY, TOYLIKE, IN THE EVEN,

HERE I SEE IT GLOW WITH DAY UNDER GLOWING HEAVEN.

child-sized orchards

Nothing is quite so majestic as a full-sized fruit tree, mature and erect, its branches dangling with ripe rewards. Picking a home-grown apple, peach, or cherry and eating it right from the tree is a pleasure too few children experience today. But getting fruit from full-sized trees can be a harrowing adventure requiring ladders or special long-handled picking devices. For children, dwarf fruit trees—more and more the choice of commercial growers—offer the simple pleasure of fresh fruit close enough to

reach. A dwarf fruit tree grows only ten to fifteen feet tall, yet it still produces full-sized fruit, often within two years of planting. A dwarf orchard is a reasonable possibility for even a small yard. Or, for a patio orchard, try miniature fruit trees, which grow only four to eight feet high, produce full-sized fruit, and can be grown in containers. Most fruit trees bear much more heavily when planted close to a different variety for cross-pollination. Try planting two varieties of apples with two of pears. *Voila!* A tiny orchard.

Apples, plums, peaches, pears, cherries, apricots, and nectarines all grow on dwarf trees. Children like to reach up and pick their favorite fruits right from the branch instead of having to use a ladder.

candy-fragrant herbs

Above left and right: Where does the smell of mint come from? Two herb choices include pineapple mint and chocolate-peppermint geranium, whose foliage is highly fragrant, especially when rubbed between the fingers.

Children may know that chocolate comes from cocoa beans and that lemons come from citrus trees. But the aroma of chocolate also comes from a particular type of geranium foliage and from the herb called chocolate mint. The tangy scent of lemon is produced by numerous herbs, including lemon balm, lemongrass, and lemon verbena. Fragrant herb gardens filled with the smells of candy, cake, fruit, lemonade, and pizza offer children the opportunity to nurture fragrances they already associate with great pleasure. Children can also learn how to make subtle olfactory distinctions by growing four types of minty herbs— pineapple mint, gingermint, spearmint, and peppermint, for example—or three types of basil, such as Fire Leaf, Purple Ruffles, and Spicy Globe. A family herb garden can also spark spicy conversations about meal preparation. Parents and children learn together which herbs are good in salads, which are great in spaghetti, which make yummy tea or add flair to cookies, and even which they can offer to the cat.

TINY WOODS BELOW WHOSE BOUGHS SHADY FAIRIES WEAVE A HOUSE;

old-time berry bushes

So many childhood memories are associated with berries. My Tennessee grandmother, Willie Norfleet, used to make a drippy blackberry jelly that she would pour over buttered biscuits as a lunchtime dessert. My Georgia grandmother, Maxie Head, made a syrupy strawberry jam that was just the right topping for her famous pound cake. Memories of berries in the garden are just as sweet. Ron Lutsko, a landscape architect, let his children plant strawberries randomly all over his backyard so that they had something to pick and eat "no matter where they landed." Most berry bushes are sold in multiples by catalogue nursery sources, so find a spot with room for five, ten, or twenty plants. Try geographically appropriate varieties of blackberry, blueberry, currant, raspberry, boysenberry, elderberry, gooseberry, or strawberry.

Opposite, top left and bottom right: Boysenberries and black-berries should be planted along a fence or trellis for support. Top right and bottom left: Straw-berries and blueberries grow in nearly any U.S. climate. Left: Thornless berry varieties are good choices for young pickers.

p i c k a b l e   p o s i e s

Adult gardens tend primarily to feature visual display. But when children visit botanical gardens and arboretums, they inevitably want to pick the flowers and collect sticks, leaves, berries, and butterflies. A good antidote to the "don't pick the flowers" rules of public gardens is to plant at home an extravagant garden with sweeping swaths of flowers meant to be picked. If children are taught to pinch off the heads of dead flowers, many annuals will be encouraged to grow even bushier. Clarkia, sweet pea, cosmos, godetia, snapdragon, salvia, zinnia, coleus, and celosia, to name just a few, are annuals that produce even more vigorously the more they are picked. Many of these flowers do not last long indoors in vases, but the simple act of picking holds the primary value for children, especially the younger ones. Display, while important, is a secondary consideration.

Above: At George Washington's River Farm, Molly Foley sneaks a few pinches of coleus, whose foliage grows denser when its tops are regularly nipped off. Opposite, clockwise from top left: Annuals that benefit from being picked—cosmos, Peter Pan white zinnia, mixed godetia, and White Star zinnia.

ALL THE NAMES I KNOW FROM NURSE:

GARDENER'S GARTERS, SHEPHERD'S PURSE,

majestic meadows

A natural meadow is a place where native flowers and grasses grow, spread, reseed, and go through the changes of natural succession—each year different from the one before. Backyard meadow gardens can be created in ways that recreate nature's effects, using native or hardy nonnative plants or a mix of the two. But families should be aware that "meadow" does not mean "maintenance free." Just like any cultivated space, a backyard meadow has to be weeded so that it does not become an overgrown eyesore. Many companies sell wildflower seed mixes, some better than others, for creating "instant meadows." Another option offering a bit more control is to plant patches of perennial and reseeding annual seedlings in naturalistic formations and let them spread.

The Davis family's meadowy garden in Salisbury, Maryland, is filled with spreading perennials and reseeding annuals, including evening primrose, blue speedwell, cranesbill, lamb's ear, catchfly, salvia, nigella, and annual poppy. For a naturalistic effect plants are allowed to "run around" the garden bed at will.

148

AND THE LADY HOLLYHOCK.

l e a r n i n g

Learning about plants becomes a game when gardens are organized around themes. Children seem to painlessly absorb history, literature, paleontology, and taxonomic botany lessons when the learning starts with stems, leaves, and blooms. Theme gardens have always been popular with adults. Medicinal gardens, fragrance gardens, color gardens (witness the fad of the white garden of the 1980s), kitchen gardens—all feed adults' need for inspired organization. Children also love theme gardens, especially when the subjects recall childhood stories, songs, lessons, or family lore. A Peter Rabbit garden planted with Mr. McGregor's beets, radishes, and strawberries brings to life a story children have heard and seen illustrated in books but not replicated with living props. A dinosaur garden provides another type of living play space, one where ancient stories blow through the leaves of mysterious bracken, horsetails, and ginkgos. A Tinkerbell garden filled with tiny fairy flowers such as cowslip, foxglove, and creeping thyme can be planted and then sprinkled with corn starch "fairy dust" for good luck. And ethnic gardens allow children to cultivate the plants and enjoy the foods of their ancestors' or friends' homelands.

Oversized plants and a friendly wood apatosaur enliven George Washington's River Farm. Here children can learn about mammoth sunflowers and fragrant lemongrass while indulging their need to climb and dig in the sand.

151

daunting dinosaurs

Dinosaurs capture the attention of children because they belong to the thrilling world of make-believe as well as the serious realm of science. A dinosaur garden is a place to play out fantasies of the lost pages of time with the help of plant materials and imagination-inspiring land forms and sculpture. At the Michigan 4-H Children's Garden, the Dinosaur Garden includes prehistoric plants, a sinuous sandbox known as a "dino dig pit," a "dino ribcage" made of steel and overgrown with vines, and a stegosaurus grown from sphagnum-form topiary. Plants that have been around since the dinosaurs include cycads, ferns, pine and gingko trees, club mosses, and horsetails. From among these choose some that will grow in your region. All require a moist, semishady planting site.

Above: Fact and fancy merge in the Dinosaur Garden of the Michigan 4-H Children's Garden. Prehistoric plants mix with stone and topiary dinosaur sculptures, a "dino dig pit" sandbox, and a "dino ribcage" arbor covered with whimsical dinosaur gourds. Opposite, clockwise from top left: Plants that lived with the dinosaurs—horsetails, ferns, club mosses, and pines.

THAT NOW YOU SMOKE YOUR PIPE AROUND,

153

p e r f o r m i n g   p l a n t s

Children are more fascinated by animals than by plants, so what better way to draw their attention to the botanical world than by introducing them to plants that act like animals? Captivating carnivores include the infamous Venus fly trap, whose mouth opens and catches insects; pitcher plants, whose "neck" has bristles in which insects become trapped; bladderworts, which trap tiny crustaceans and water insects; butterworts, cobra lilies, and sundew. While probably no other plant can beat the Venus fly trap for drama, many others put on a show for children in less lethal ways. A garden of performing plants includes botanical wonders that visibly, physically do something. The Michigan 4-H Children's Garden has a cast of performing plants that do everything from repel mosquitoes to close their branchlets on a finger when touched. Here are some stars.

Right top: The Venus fly trap's nectar lures insects into its lethal jaws. Bottom: Chinese lanterns were named for their papery orange pods. Opposite, top: Money plant seed pods are perfect to pick and "spend." Bottom: The mimosa's sensitive branchlets fold up when touched.

GREAT PERFORMANCES

Balloon flower *(Platycodon grandiflorus 'Komachi')*: its blossoms are shaped like balloons

Chinese lantern *(Physalis alkekengi)*: its stems produce wispy, bright orange lanterns

Compass plant *(Silphium laciniatum)*: its leaves orient north and south

Cup plant *(Silphium perfoliatum)*: its leaves form a cup that traps water

Gas plant *(Dictamnus albus)*: its flowers release a gas at night that can be lighted

Love-in-a-puff *(Cardiospermum halicacabum)*: its puffy pods contain heart-marked seeds

Money plant *(Lunaria annua)*: its papery seed cases look like coins

Mosquito plant *(Agastache rupestris)*: it may repel mosquitoes

Obedient plant *(Physostegia virginiana)*: its flowers, when twisted on their stems, stay in place

Sensitive plant *(Mimosa pudica)*: its branchlets fold up when touched

Snapdragon *(Antirrhinum majus)*: it snaps like jaws when the flower base is squeezed

Tufted hair grass *(Deschampsia caespitosa 'Fairy's Joke')*: its clumps are weighed down with tiny plantlets instead of seeds

timeless sundials

Sundial gardens, created from plants that open and close at various times of the day in accordance with the sun's rays, are an old favorite among seasoned gardeners. At the Michigan 4-H Children's Garden, the Sundial Garden allows a child to become a living sundial gnomon: he can stand on a paved spot, throw his arms up in the air, and cast a shadow on the ground that will point to a number on the human-scale clock sculpted into the ground and adorned with a bas-relief brass sun sculpture at its center. Making a garden like this is a beautiful way to teach children how to tell time.

Footprints pressed into concrete in the center of the Sundial Garden at the Michigan 4-H Children's Garden show children where to stand at different times of the year to correctly cast a time-telling shadow.

156

A GARDEN OF TIME

Coreopsis: Moonbeam, a lemon-yellow flower; Sunray, an orange-yellow flower

Evening primrose: Tina James, flowers that open within fifteen seconds of sunset

Four-o'-clock: flowers that open at about 4 p.m.

Moonflower: flowers that open only after sunset

Morning glory: flowers that open only in the morning

Sunflower: Teddy Bear, a sunny yellow flower

Thyme: a ground-covering pun on "time"

Left top: Moonbeam coreopsis creates a cheerful border for a garden of time. Bottom: Fast-growing, vigorous morning glories are famous for opening at the break of day and closing as the sun sets in the west.

An alphabet garden, one of the simplest theme gardens for children, is a living lesson in both the ABCs and flower names. Go through a plant catalogue with children to find plants that start with each alphabet letter. (Parents will have to prune children's decisions for climate, sun, and soil conditions, of course). To start, lay out a planting bed with markers for each letter. Alongside each marker, plant flowers that start with that letter. Choose several plants of each variety to make a strong sensory statement and allow for plenty of picking. Use as many perennials as possible, so that the children have a real sense of continuity and growth in the alphabet garden over the years.

Making an alphabet garden is as simple as ABC. At George Washington's River Farm, craft-store wooden letters were placed in the planting beds in order from A for aster to Z for zinnia.

Aster

Balloon flower

Catmint

Daisy

Eggplant

Forget-me-not

Goldenrod

Hen and chicks

Ice plant

Johnny-jump-up

Kale

Lamb's ear

Milkweed

Nasturtium

Obedient plant

Pussy toes

Queen Anne's lace

Rosemary

Snow in summer

Turtlehead

Unicorn plant

Violet

Wormwood

Xeranthemum

Yarrow

Zinnia

tinkerbell gardens

Children love to pretend that the world is full of magic, so creating an enchanted garden together may be just what the fairy godmother ordered. Herbalists across the United States are beginning to revive an ancient custom: the planting of gardens associated with fairy lore. Certain plants have, through the centuries, been mentioned over and over in fairy tales. Creeping thyme, for example, is a favorite hiding place during daylight hours, the time fairies prefer to sleep. Fairy bells, tiny bell-shaped flowers, are well suited for fairy musical needs, and fairy cups make perfect shelter during rain showers. Fairy favorites include apple trees, blue flax, contorted hazlenut trees, cowslip, creeping thyme, elder, ferns, forget-me-not, foxglove, hawthorn, heartsease, hollyhock, lily-of-the-valley, mallow, narcissus, oak trees, rosemary, St. Johnswort, and tulips.

A fairy garden on the edge of the Burroughs family's backyard woods in Ashton, Maryland, creates magic with scores of pale pink and white flower varieties—including these stunning foxgloves—along with plants selected for their enchanting silver and gold foliage.

WE MAY SEE HOW ALL THINGS ARE, SEAS AND CITIES, NEAR AND FAR,

h u n g r y   p e t e r   r a b b i t s

What child cannot identify with Peter Rabbit, Beatrix Potter's infamous little hero whose curious nibblings and scamperings in Mr. McGregor's garden constantly get him into trouble? The Peter Rabbit Garden at the Michigan 4-H Children's Garden in East Lansing has a tiny gate, like the one Peter squeezed under to enter Mr. McGregor's forbidden garden, and on it hangs a tiny blue jacket with brass buttons, like the one Peter lost. On the sidewalk around the garden are imprints of little scampering rabbit feet and giant Wellington boot prints chasing after them. The garden includes many of the berries, vegetables, and herbs mentioned in the Beatrix Potter stories: strawberries (Pink Panda), beets (McGregor's Favorite), radishes (French Breakfast), and rhubarb (Valentine), as well as chamomile, hyssop, lavender, lemon balm, mint, parsley, rosemary, sage, and tansy.

Surrounded by chamomile and lavender, Peter Rabbit munches a carrot snatched from Mr. McGregor's garden. Peter's little blue jacket, lost during the course of his vegetable theft, hangs on a child-sized gate.

s e a   g a r d e n s

On the asphalt playground of
Hotwell Primary School, in the
port city of Bristol, England,
the landscape architect Nancy
Copplestone has designed a sea
garden of plants that define the
old city's watery edges: Bristol
onion (allium), flower of Bristol,
jungle bamboo, sea holly, spiked
speedwell, thrift or sea pink, and
white-leafed rock rose. These she
planted on an underused area
of the playground in raised beds
with undulating wooden borders
to represent waves. The remaining
asphalt was painted with sprightly
images of fish, sea horses, and
octopuses. The result? A drab
playground transformed into a
serene outdoor learning and play
space. Copplestone's approach
can be adapted in any town
or city with a local waterway by
researching native plant materials,
local plant history, and folklore.

**A garden of plants native to the
banks of old Bristol's Avon River
Gorge transforms a primary
school's sterile asphalt playground into a lush place for rest
or play. Here lessons about en-
dangered native plants are easy
to absorb. Holding it all in is
a fence as wavy as the sea.**

In the classic Oz novels and film, plants make their way into the story line more than once. In one of the more harrowing scenes, Dorothy, Toto, and the Cowardly Lion nearly die in a field of poppies that lull them into unconsciousness. They are saved by the Tin Woodsman and the Scarecrow, who withstand the effect of the poppies because they are not actual living creatures. A simple garden of Green Wizard or Toto black-eyed Susans, poppies (any variety), and Munchkin, Oz, or Wizard pumpkins, all planted in abundance, can be the most magical a child ever experiences. Do not forget to lay a sinuous yellow brick path through the middle, as can be found in the Scarecrow Garden at the Michigan 4-H Children's Garden.

Left top and bottom: Two magical choices for a Wizard of Oz garden include Toto black-eyed Susans and a miniature meadow of bright red poppies. Put up a scarecrow in one corner, a lion sculpture in another; make a curving yellow path, and the backyard becomes the land of Oz.

earthy fragrances

Today most of the scents that fill everyday lives are created and prepackaged by manufacturers. A 1992 study by the environmental researcher A. R. Hirsch asked people to report what smells caused them to become nostalgic. Those born in the three decades before 1940 noted the aroma of pine, roses, fish, manure, honeysuckle, hay, clover, and burning leaves, while people born in the 1960s and 1970s mentioned PlayDo, chlorine, crayons, Downy, SweeTarts, baby aspirin, mothballs, and scented magic markers. An alternative repertoire of everyday smells can be provided by a garden filled with unusual, intense and pleasant fragrances. The Perfume Garden of the Michigan 4-H Children's Garden includes perfume basil, Munstead lavender, lemon mint, mountain mint, clove pinks, spice shrub, evening scented stock, rosemary, Galica rose, and mignonette—sweet smells all.

Right: Fragrant Munstead lavender defines the edge of the Perfume Garden at the Michigan 4-H Children's Garden. Parents can create a similar plot for their own children by including rosemary, spice shrub, and evening scented stock as well.

Above: Lavender has long been used by the fragrance industry to make everything from perfume to bath oil to sachets. Its beautiful color and subtle fragrance make it one of the most popular garden plants as well.

Planting gardens with trees, herbs, vegetables, and flowers common to an ancestral homeland can be a great sensory lesson for children about their roots. Many public gardens in this country have such plots, sometimes called rainbow gardens, that reflect America's multifaceted ethnic heritage. A family can create a garden that celebrates its own heritage by finding out what plants are common to its homeland. Visit the botany section of the local public library, or contact the closest botanical garden or university botany department for appropriate suggestions. Also keep in mind the climate of origin. Here are a few examples of ethnic gardens from the New York Botanical Garden.

At the New York Botanical Garden, every year neighborhood residents take turns planting, tending, and harvesting family gardens with plants that grow in their own homelands. Gardens of Russia, Mexico, Vietnam, Nigeria, and the Caribbean islands are just a few that have been cultivated.

Above: In the New York Botanical Garden's Chinese family garden, a boy harvests a giant zucchini. Right: In the African garden, bananas and pineapples grow together with marigold, salvia, and impatiens. A scarecrow sports Nigerian garb.

THE SONGS YOU SING, THE TALES YOU TELL,

CHINESE GARDEN

Flowers: amaranth, camellia, China aster, clematis, gardenia, hollyhock, hydrangea, peony

Fruits: cherry

Vegetables: bitter melon, bok choy, Chinese celery, cucumber, eggplant, string beans, winter melon

Herbs: garlic, garlic chives

Other: bottle gourd, tea, walnut tree

AFRICAN GARDEN

Flowers and foliage plants: African violet, amaranth, bird-of-paradise, caladium, freesia, impatiens, lobelia, marigold, pelargonium, salvia

Fruits: calabash, paw-paw, banana, pineapple

Vegetables: cassava, Ceylon spinach, cow peas, okra, yams

Herbs: bitterleaf, ginger, sansevieria, waterleaf

resources

pp. 11–12: Impact of outdoor spaces on child development. Mark Francis and Randolph Hester, *The Meaning of Gardens: Idea, Place, and Action* (Cambridge, Mass.: MIT Press, 1990).

pp. 12, 23, 108, 126, 148: Children's loss of knowledge of the natural world, the necessity of wild places. Gary Paul Nabhan and Stephen Trimble, *The Geography of Childhood: Why Children Need Wild Places* (Boston: Beacon Press, 1994).

p. 12: Children's need for physical experiences in nature. Robin C. Moore, *Childhood's Domain* (London: Croom Helm, 1986; reprint, Berkeley, Calif.: MIG Communications, 1990).

p. 12: Nature helps sick people. Roger S. Ulrich, "View Through a Window May Influence Recovery from Surgery," *Science* 224 (1984): 420–21. Bernadine E. Cimprich, "Attentional Fatigue and Restoration in Individuals with Cancer" (Ph.D. diss., University of Michigan, 1990).

p. 12: Natural setting reduces stress. Rachel Kaplan and Stephen Kaplan, *The Experience of Nature: A Psychological Perspective* (New York: Cambridge University Press, 1989). Roger S. Ulrich, "Stress Recovery During Exposure to Natural and Urban Environments," *Journal of Environmental Psychology* 11 (1991): 201–30.

p. 12: Complex environments increase intelligence. Marion Cleeves Diamond, "The Morphological Cortical Changes as a Consequence of Learning and Experience," in *Neurobiology of Higher Cognitive Functions*, eds. A. B. Scheibel and A. F. Wechsler (New York: Gilford Press, 1990), 1–10.

pp. 12–13: Human anxieties and preferences. Roger S. Ulrich, "Biophilia, Biophobia, and Natural Landscapes," in *The Biophilia Hypothesis*, eds. Stephen R. Kellert and Edward O. Wilson (Washington, D.C.: Island Press, 1993), 73–137.

p. 13: "so dependent on the organizing side of our brain . . ." Interview with Charles Lewis, author of *Green Nature, Human Nature: The Meaning of Plants in Our Lives* (Champaign: University of Illinois Press, 1996).

p. 13: "biologically prepared learning . . ." Gary Paul Nabhan and Sara St. Antoine, "The Loss of Floral and Faunal Story: The Extinction of Experience," in *The Biophilia Hypothesis*, eds. Stephen R. Kellert and Edward O. Wilson (Washington, D.C.: Island Press, 1993), 229–50.

p. 14: For a summary of Froebel's ideas, see J. L. Hughes, *Froebel's Educational Laws for All Teachers* (New York: D. Appleton, 1897). See also Norman Brosterman, *Inventing Kindergarten* (New York: Abrams, 1997).

pp. 14–15: History of playground development. Joe L. Frost, *Play and Playscapes* (Albany, N.Y.: Delmar, 1992), 115.

p. 15: "spade, rake, hoe. . . " Gertrude Jekyll, *Children and Gardens* (1908; reprint, Suffolk, England: Antique Collector's Club, 1982), 22.

p. 17: "an informal outdoor living room . . ." Thomas Church, *Gardens Are for People* (Berkeley, Calif.: University of California Press, 1995), ix.

p. 18: "the greatest physical joy . . ." Henry Mitchell, "Watery Rewards," *Washington Post Magazine*, 2 May 1993, 33.

pp. 18, 20: Children's reactions to water and animals. Monica Buntin Myhill, "What Kids Really Want in a Garden for Children: Fact vs. Fiction" (paper presented at the AHS Children's Gardening Symposium, Callaway Gardens, Ga., June 1996).

pp. 18–23: Children's responses to garden settings. Catherine Eberbach, "Children's Gardens: The Meaning of Place," *The Role of Horticulture in Human Well-Being and Social Development*, ed. Diane Relf (Portland, Ore.: Timber Press, 1992), 80–83.

pp. 18–23: Garden design elements fascinating to children. Eberbach, "Garden Design for Children" (master's thesis, University of Delaware, 1988).

pp. 20, 72–82, 97–103: Prospect-refuge theory. Jay Appleton, *The Experience of Landscape* (New York: Wiley, 1996).

pp. 20, 87–95: Loose parts theory. Simon Nicholson, "How Not to Cheat Children: The Theory of Loose Parts," *Landscape Architecture Quarterly*, October 1971, 30.

p. 23: Schoolyards as the last communal outdoor spaces. Mary S. Rivkin, *The Great Outdoors: Restoring Children's Right to Play Outside* (Washington, D.C.: National Association for the Education of Young Children, 1995).

p. 23: Nature affiliation established in childhood. Roger Hart, *Children's Experience of Place* (New York: Irvington, 1979).

pp. 25, 128, 136, 138, 156, 158: Theme gardens. Sharon Lovejoy, *Sunflower Houses: Garden Discoveries for Children of All Ages* (Loveland, Colo.: Interweave Press, 1991).

p. 26: Shrub barriers. Bunny Guinness, *Creating a Family Garden* (Abbeville Press, 1996). Robin C. Moore, *Plants for Play: A Plant Selection Guide for Children's Outdoor Environments* (Berkeley, Calif.: MIG Communications, 1993), 56.

p. 26: Ornamental grasses. Interview with Kurt Bluemel, proprietor of a foremost ornamental grass nursery; see also Kurt Bluemel Wholesale Nursery Catalogue.

pp. 27, 119: Plants that take abuse; plants for path crevices. Gordon Hayward, *Garden Paths: Inspiring Designs and Practical Projects* (Charlotte, Vt.: Camden House, 1993), 214.

pp. 27–28: Poisonous plants. Moore, *Plants for Play*, 74–82.

pp. 27–28: Toxic plant parts. Brian Capon, *Botany for Gardeners* (Portland, Ore.: Timber Press, 1990), 93–98.

p. 28: Natural alternatives to barbed wire. Moore, *Plants for Play*, 55.

p. 29: Hazards and challenges. Robin C. Moore, Susan Goltsman, and Daniel Iacofano, eds. *Play for All Guidelines: Planning, Design, and Management of Outdoor Play Settings for All Children* (Berkeley, Calif.: MIG Communications, 1992), 10.

p. 63: "restores the ecology of our own backyards . . ." Sara Stein, *Noah's Garden: Restoring the Ecology of Our Own Backyards* (New York: Houghton Mifflin, 1993).

p. 66: Garden configurations for birds. Guinness, *Creating a Family Garden*.

p. 160: Fairy lore. Jane Hogue, *Gardens That Children Will Dig!* (n.d.). Betsy Williams, *Are There Fairies at the Bottom of Your Garden?* (n.d.).

p. 164: Nostalgia-producing odors. Rivkin, *The Great Outdoors*, p. 10.

featured designers

Jo Bemis
Island Fine Arts Ltd
53 High Street
Bembridge
Isle of Wight PO35 5SE, England
011-44-1983-87-5133
gallery@islandfinearts.com
www.islandfinearts.com
Page 80 bottom left

Lheena Bhimani
6910 Courageous Circle
Burke, VA 22015
703-455-1242
Pages 158–59

Alastair Bolton
Page 8

Karen Burroughs
7462 Mink Hollow Road
Ashton, MD 20861
301-854-0015
Page 160

Campbell & Ferrara Design
6651 Little River Turnpike
Alexandria, VA 22312
703-354-6724
info@cambellferrara.com
www.campbellferrara.com
Pages 52–53

Alex Champion
Earth Symbols
P.O. Box 145
Philo, CA 95466
707-895-3375
earthsymbols@earthlink.net
www.earthsymbols.com
Page 123 right

Nancy Copplestone
10 Goldney Avenue
Clifton
Bristol BS8 4RA, England
011-44-117-946-6899
Page 162

Mary Palmer Dargan
Hugh Dargan Associates
P.O. Box 11730
Atlanta, GA 30355
404-231-3889
info@dargan.com
www.dargan.com
Page 106–7

Topher Delaney
600 Illinois Street
San Francisco, CA 94107
415-621-9899
tdelaney@tdelaney.com
www.tdelaney.com
Page 118 top right

DLM Design
Page 74

Patrick Dougherty
9007 Dodson's Crossroad
Chapel Hill, NC 27516
919-967-6533
stickwork@earthlink.net
www.stickwork.net
Page 80 top left

Kenneth S. Duffy
Geoscape
P.O. Box 552
Merrifield, VA 22116
703-716-5660
info@geoscapeinc.com
www.geoscapeinc.com
Pages 56–57, 61, 64, 69

Catherine Eberbach
Center for Learning in Out of School
Environments
University of Pittsburgh
3933 O'Hara Street, First Floor
Pittsburgh, PA 15260
412-624-7477
cle4@pitt.edu
Pages 9,17,140–41, 166–69

Fred Ellman
Roundtable Design
1672 East Seventh Street
Brooklyn, NY 11230
718-645-4191, 914-591-7640
Pages 88, 94, 102

Trudi Entwistle
011-44-798-029-5538
Trudi@trudientwistle.com
www.trudientwistle.com
Pages 80 bottom left, 81

Adrian Fisher Mazes Ltd.
Portman Lodge
Durweston
Glandford Forum
Dorset DT110QA, England
702-733-7722
sales@mazemaker.com
www.mazemaker.com
Pages 122–23

Isabelle Greene and Associates
2613 De la Vina Street
Santa Barbara, CA 93105
805-569-4045
iga@isabellegreene.com
www.gballiance.comisabellegreene.html
Pages 38–43, 60

Jane Hogue
Prairie Pedlar
1609 270th Street
Odebolt, IA 51458
712-668-4840
jhogue@netins.net
http://showcase.netins.net/web/ppgarden/
Pages 67, 71, 128–29, 136–37

Enid Hubbard
Page 70

Raymond Jungles and Debra Yates
Raymond Jungles Incorporated
242 SW Fifth Street
Miami, FL 33130
305-858-6777
Raymond@raymondjungles.com
www.raymondjungles.com
Pages 44–49, 79, 90–91, 108, 112

Jeffrey Kacos and Deborah Kinney
4-H Children's Garden
Department of Horticulture
A240-B Plant and Soil Science Building
Michigan State University
East Lansing, MI 48824
517-432-5657
4hgarden@msue.msu.edu
http://4hgarden.msu.edu
Pages 103, 113, 120, 121, 127, 134 top and
bottom, 152, 156, 161, 164–65

Erik Katzmaier
Katzmaier, Newell, Kerr
2728 East Coast Highway
Corona Del Mar, CA 92625
949-760-0454
Pages 110, 111

Harley Kelley
Pages 38–39, 40 right

Larry Kirkland
5721 Utah Avenue, NW
Washington, DC 20015
202-244-8489
Pages 116–17

Jim Long
Long Creek Herbs
P.O. Box 127
Blue Eye, MO 65611
417-779-5450
LCHerbs@interline.net
www.Longcreekherbs.com
Page 129 left

Doug Macy
Walker Macy
111 S.W. Oak Street, Suite 200
Portland, OR 97204
503-228-3122
inform@WalkerMacy.com
www.walkermacy.com
Pages 116–17

Sasa Marinkov
Orleans Infant School
Hartington Road, Twickenham
Middlesex TWI 3EN, England
011-44-181-892-1654
Page 130 top

Steve Martino and Associates
111 East Dunlap Avenue
Suite 1-625
Phoenix, AZ 85020
602-957-6150
www.stevemartino.net
Page 21

Gail Michaud
Pages 66, 82, 104–5

Oehme, van Sweden and Associates
800 G Street, SE
Washington, DC 20003
202-546-7575
cturner@ovsla.com
www.ovsla.com
Pages 93 right, 126–27

Outback Design
Pages 84–85

Lynn Richard and Sarah Tolford
Brookside Gardens
1800 Glenallan Avenue
Wheaton, MD 20902
301-962-1400
ellen.hartranft@mncppc-mc.org
www.mc-mncppc.org/parks/brookside
Page 131

Jack Rogers
Bow House
P.O. Box 900
Bolton, MA 01741
978-779-6464
info@bowhouse.com
www.bowhouse.com
Page 174

Luke Salaman
St. Werberg's Park Nursery School
Glenfrome Road
Bristol BS2 9UX, England
011-44-117-955-6380
Page 130 bottom

Herb Schaal
EDAW
240 East Mountain Avenue
Fort Collins, CO 80524
970-484-6073
www.edaw.com

Noranne Scott
c/o Trudi Entwistle
011-44-798-029-5538
Trudi@trudientwistle.com
www.trudientwistle.com

Shimizu Landscape Corporation
6101 Bryn Mawr Avenue
Glen Echo. MD 20812
301-229-9483l
Page 81 bottom right

Simple Horticultural Art Gallery
1397 East Main Street
Douglassville, PA 19518
610-404-1760
simple@simplegardenart.com
http://www.simplegardenart.com
Pages 22 bottom, 124

Snitzer Landscaping
P.O. Box 38
Dickerson, MD 20842
301-428-8310
Page 75 top and bottom

Jane Taylor
6132 Shoeman Road
Haslett, MI 48840
517-655-1912
Pages 103, 113, 120, 121, 127, 134 top
and bottom, 152, 156, 161, 164–65, 165

Faik Tugberk
Architects Collaborative
9400 Old Georgetown Road
Bethesda, MD 20814
301-897 9000
Page 83

Kibbe Turner
Wildlife Habitats
P.O. Box 420
New Market, MD 21774
301-831-9217
Pages 59, 65, 93 left

Andrew Wenchel
305 North Kenmore Street
Arlington, VA 22201
703 521 3021
afwenchel@comcast.net
Pages 114–15

Kathy Wheeler
Pages 158–59

organizations

American Community Gardening Association
c/o Franklin Park Conservatory
1777 East Broad Street
Columbus, OH 43203
877-275-2242
www.communitygarden.org

American Horticultural Society
7931 East Boulevard Drive
Alexandria, VA 22308
703-768-5700
www.ahs.org

American Public Gardens Association
100 West Tenth Street
Suite 614
Wilmington, DE 19801
302-655-7100
www.publicgardens.org

Center for Ecoliteracy
2528 San Pablo Avenue
Berkeley, CA 94702
info@ecoliteracy.org
www.ecoliteracy.org

Hobby Greenhouse Association
2049 Baughman Road
Jeannette, PA 15644
www.hobbygreenhouse.org

Institute for Ecosystem Studies
Ecosystem Literacy Initiative
P.O. Box R
Millbrook, NY 12545
845-677-5343
www.ecostudies.org/eli.html

Kids Gardening
National Gardening Association
1100 Dorset Street
South Burlington, VT 05403
800-538-7476
www.kidsgardening.org

Lady Bird Johnson National Wildflower Center
4801 La Crosse Avenue
Austin, TX 78739
512-292-4100
www.wildflower.org

Learning Through Landscapes
Southside Offices
Third Floor
The Law Courts
Winchester
Hampshire SO23 9DL, England
011-44-196-284-5811
www.ltl.org.uk

LifeLab Science Program
1156 High Street
Santa Cruz, CA 95064
831-459-2001
www.lifelab.org

National Agriculture in the Classroom
U.S. Department of Agriculture
Cooperative State Research
Education and Extension Service
1400 Independence Avenue, SW
Stop 2251
Washington, DC 20250-2251
202-720-2727
www.agclassroom.org

National 4-H Council
7100 Connecticut Avenue
Chevy Chase, MD 20815
301-961-2800
www.fourhcouncil.edu

National Gardening Association
1100 Dorset Street
South Burlington, VT 05403
802-863-1308
http://assoc.garden.org/about

National Junior Master Gardener Program
225 Horticulture/Forestry Building
Texas A&M University
College Station, TX 77843-2134
979-845-8565
http://jmgkids.us

National Wildlife Federation
11100 Wildlife Center Drive
Reston, VA 20190
800-822-9919
www.nwf.org

New England Wild Flower Society Inc.
Garden in the Woods
180 Hemenway Road
Framingham, MA 01701
508-877-7630
http://newfs.org

People-Plant Council
Office of Environmental Horticulture
407 Saunders Hall
Blacksburg, VA 24061
540-231-6254
www.hort.vt.edu

Project Wild
Council for Environmental Education
5555 Morningside
Suite 212
Houston, TX 77005
713-520-1936
www.projectwild.org

The Rodale Institute
611 Siegfriedale Road
Kutztown, PA 19530-9320
610-683-1400
www.rodaleinstitute.org

Seed Savers Exchange
3094 North Winn Road
Decorah, IA 52101
563-382-5990
www.seedsavers.org

Treeture Environmental Education Program
4 Hamilton Road
Scarsdale, NY 10583
www.treetures.com

Young Entomologists' Society
Minibeast Zooseum and Education Center
6907 West Grand River Avenue
Lansing, MI 48906-9131
517-886-0630
http://members.aol.com/YESbugs/mainmenu.html

children's gardens

Atlanta Botanical Garden
1345 Piedmont Avenue, NE
Atlanta, GA 30309
404-876-5859
info@atlantabotanicalgarden.org
www.atlantabotanicalgarden.org

Brooklyn Botanic Garden
1000 Washington Avenue
Brooklyn, NY 11225
718-623-7200
http://bbg.org

Brookside Gardens
1800 Glenallen Avenue
Wheaton, MD 20902
301-962-1400
www.mc-mncppc.org/parks/brookside

Camden Children's Garden
3 Riverside Drive
Camden, NJ 08103
856-365-8733
www.camdenchildrensgarden.org

Cantigny Park
1 South 151 Winfield Road
Wheaton, IL 60187
630-668-5161
www.cantignypark.com

Cleveland Botanical Garden
11030 East Boulevard
Cleveland, OH 44106
216-721-1600
info@cbgarden.org
www.cbgarden.org

George Washington's River Farm
7931 East Boulevard Drive
Alexandria, VA 22308
800-777-7931, 703-768-5700
info@ahs.org
www.ahs.org

Green Bay Botanical Garden
2600 Larsen Road
Green Bay, WI 54307
920-490-9457
info@gbbg.org
www.gbbg.org

Hershey Gardens
170 Hotel Road
Hershey, PA 17033
717-534-3492
www.hersheygardens.org

Hilltop Garden and Nature Center
2301 East Tenth Street
Bloomington, IN 47405
812-855-2799
hilltop@indiana.edu
www.indiana.edu/~hilltop

The Huntington Botanical Gardens
1151 Oxford Road
San Marino, CA 91108
626-405-2100
www.huntington.org

Ithaca Children's Garden
615 Willow Avenue
Ithaca, NY 14850
607-272-2292
http://counties.cce.cornell.edu/tompkins/
ithacachildrensgarden

Leila Arboretum Society
928 West Michigan Avenue
Battle Creek, MI 49017
269-969-0270, ext 119
www.leilaarboretumsociety.org

Lewis Ginter Botanical Garden
1800 Lakeside Avenue
Richmond, VA 23228
804-262-9887
www.lewisginter.org

Longwood Gardens
Route One
Kennett Square, PA 19348
610-388-1000
http://longwoodgardens.com

Michigan 4-H Children's Garden
Michigan State University
Department of Horticulture
Plant and Soil Sciences Building
East Lansing, MI 48824
517-432-5657
4hgarden@msue.msu.edu
http://4hgarden.msu.edu

Missouri Botanical Garden
4344 Shaw Boulevard
St. Louis, MO 63110
314-577-9400
www.mobot.org

Morton Arboretum
4100 Illinois Route 53
Lisle, IL 60532
630-968-0074
trees@mortonarb.org
www.mortonarb.org

New York Botanical Garden
200th Street and Southern Boulevard
Bronx, NY 10458
718-817-8700
www.nybg.org

Norfolk Botanical Garden
6700 Azalea Garden Road
Norfolk, VA 23518
757-441-5830
www.norfolkbotanicalgarden.org

Phipps Conservatory and Botanical Gardens
One Schenley Park
Frank Curto Drive
Pittsburgh, PA 15219
412-622-6915
phipps@phipps.pgh.pa.us
www./phipps.conservatory.org

San Francisco Botanical Garden
Ninth Avenue at Lincoln Way
San Francisco, CA 94122
415-661-1316
www.sfbotanicalgarden.org

U.S. National Arboretum
3501 New York Avenue, NE
Washington, DC 20002
202-245-2726
www.usna.usda.gov/

Winterthur Museum and Country Estate
Route 52
Wilmington, DE 19735
800-448-3883
www.winterthur.org

b o o k s

FOR CHILDREN

Blue Potatoes, Orange Tomatoes.
Rosalind Creasy. San Francisco: Sierra Club
Books for Children, 1994.

The Children's Kitchen Garden.
Georgeanne and Ethel Brennan. Berkeley,
Calif.: Ten Speed Press, 1997.

**Dig, Plant, Grow: A Kid's Guide
to Gardening.** Felder Rushing. Franklin,
Tenn.: Cool Springs Press, 2004.

The Gardening Book. Jane Bull. New
York: DK Children, 2003.

Gardening Wizardry for Kids.
L. Patricia Kite and Yvette Santiago Banek.
Hauppage, N.Y.: Barron's Educational
Series, 1995.

Good Bugs for Your Garden.
Allison Mia Starcher. Chapel Hill, N.C.:
Algonquin Books, 1995.

**Green Thumbs: A Kid's Activity Guide
to Indoor and Outdoor Gardening.**
Laurie Carlson. Chicago: Chicago Review
Press, 1995.

**A Harvest of Color: Growing a
Vegetable Garden.** Melanie Eclare.
Brooklyn, N.Y.: Ragged Bear Press, 2002.

**KidsGardening: A Kids' Guide to
Messing Around in the Dirt.** Kevin
Raftery and Kim Gilbert Raftery. Palo Alto,
Calif.: Klutz Press, 1989.

**New Junior Garden Book: Cool
Projects for Kids to Make and Grow.**
Felder Rushing and Wane Vincent. Des
Moines, Iowa: Better Homes and Gardens
Books, 1999.

**Roots, Shoots, Buckets and Boots:
Gardening Together with Children.**
Sharon Lovejoy. New York: Workman, 1999.

**Sunflower Houses: Inspiration from
the Garden.** Sharon Lovejoy. New York:
Workman, 2001.

Victory Garden Kids' Book. Marjorie
Waters. Old Saybrook, Conn.: Globe Pequot
Press, 1988.

FOR ADULTS

**Beyond Ecophobia: Reclaiming the
Heart in Nature Education.** David
Sobel. Great Barrington, Mass.: Orion
Society, 2005.

The Biophilia Hypothesis. Stephen R.
Kellert and Edward O. Wilson, eds.
Washington, D.C.: Island Press, 1993.

Children and Gardens. Gertrude Jekyll.
1908. Reprint, Woodbridge, England:
Antique Collector's Club, 1994.

**Children and Nature: Psychological,
Sociocultural, and Evolutionary
Investigations.** Peter H. Kahn Jr. and
Stephen R. Kellert. Cambridge, Mass.:
MIT Press, 2002.

**Children's Gardens: Twelve Theme
Gardens for Families.** Edwin L. Howard
and Richard L. Franklin. Yardley, Pa.:
Westholme, 2006.

**A Child's Garden: Introducing Your
Child to the Joys of the Garden.**
Elizabeth St. Cloud Muse. New York:
Little Brown, 2002.

Creating a Family Garden. Bunny
Guinness. New York: Abbeville, 1991.

**Ecological Literacy: Educating Our
Children for a Sustainable World.**
Michael Stone and Zenobia Barlow. San
Francisco: Sierra Club Books, 2005.

Gardening with Children. Monika
Hanneman, Patricia Hulse, Brian Johnson,
and Barbara Kurland. Brooklyn Botanic
Garden All-Region Guide. Brooklyn, N.Y.:
Brooklyn Botanic Garden, 2007.

Gardening with Children.
Beth Richardson. Newtown, Conn.:
Taunton Press, 1998.

**The Geography of Childhood:
Why Children Need Wild Places.**
Gary Paul Nabhan and Stephen Trimble.
Boston: Beacon Press, 1994.

Great Gardens for Kids. Clare
Matthews. London: Hamlyn Books, 2002.

**The Great Outdoors: Restoring
Children's Right to Play Outside.**
Mary S. Rivkin. Washington, D.C.:
National Association for the Education
of Young Children, 1995.

**Green Nature, Human Nature:
The Meaning of Plants in Our Lives.**
Charles Lewis. Champaign: University
of Illinois Press, 1996.

**Hershey Children's Garden:
Place to Grow.** Maureen Heffernan.
Athens: Ohio University Press, 2004.

**Into the Field: A Guide to Locally
Focused Teaching.** Leslie Clare Walker.
Great Barrington, Mass.: Orion Society,
2005.

Inventing Kindergarten. Norman
Brosterman. New York: Abrams, 1997.

**Last Child in the Woods: Saving Our
Children from Nature-Deficit Disorder.**
Richard Louv. Chapel Hill, N.C.: Algonquin
Books, 2006.

**The Meaning of Gardens: Idea, Place,
and Action.** Mark Francis and Randolph
Hester. Cambridge, Mass.: MIT Press, 1990.

**Place-Based Education: Connecting
Classrooms and Communities.**
David Sobel. Great Barrington, Mass.:
Orion Society, 2004.

**Plants for Play: A Plant Selection
Guide for Children's Outdoor
Environments.** Robin C. Moore. Berkeley,
Calif.: MIG Communications, 1993.

**Ready, Set, Grow: A Guide to
Gardening with Children.** Suzanne
Frutig Bales. Hoboken, N.J.: Wiley, 1996.

Sharing Nature with Children. Joseph
Bharat Cornell. 1978. Reprint, Nevada City,
Calif.: Dawn Publications, 1998.

**Treehouses: The Art and Craft
of Living Out on a Limb.** Peter Nelson.
Boston: Houghton Mifflin, 1994.

illustration credits

Bob Adler: 138

Larry Albee, Longwood Gardens: 9, 72–73

Eric R. Berndt, Photo Network: 23

Bottmann–UPI/Corbis: 16 both

James Bleecker: 14

Sharon Bradley-Papp: 34, 47

Gay Bumgarner, Photo Network: 118 bottom right

Tori Butt, New York Botanical Garden: 166–67, 168 left

Alex Champion: 123 right

Kindra Clineff, Tony Stone Images: 142

Wendy Corresl: 20, 86–87, 144 bottom left

Crandall and Crandall: 119, 139 bottom right

Molly Dannenmaier: 13, 65, 74, 114–15, 118 top and bottom left, 126–27, 127 right, 129 right, 130–31, 156, 162

Mary Palmer Dargan: 106–7

Delaney, Cochran and Castillo: 118 top right

Joel Dexter, Unicorn: 6–7

Paul Dieter: 101 right

Patrick Dougherty/Jerry Hardman Jones: 80 top left

Christine M. Douglas: 17, 77 both, 88, 94, 96–97, 99 top right, bottom left and right; 102, 140–41, 153 top right, bottom left and right; 168–69

Ken Druse, NSG: 63

Todd Eberle: 21

Trudi Entwistle: 80 bottom left and right, 81

Esbin-Anderson, Photo Network: 140 left

Adrian Fisher: 122–23

Roger Foley: 12, 30–31, 35 bottom right, 36–37, 37 right, 55, 58, 64, 68, 69, 120–21, 146, 148–49, 160

Bruce A. Fox, Michigan State University Relations: 120 left, 121 right, 152, 164–65, 165 right

Hameed Gorani: 35 top left and right

Kate Greenaway (*Children and Gardens*, by Gertrude Jekyll, courtesy of the Victoria and Albert Museum): 15

Isabelle Greene: 60

Astraea Haskin, Michigan State University Relations: 113, 133, 134 both

HDRA, Ryton Organic Gardens: 80 top right

Mary Hicks for Isabelle Greene and Associates: 43

B. W. Hoffman, Unicorn: 145

Timothy Hursley: 129 left

Dency Kane: 2, 8, 26, 52–53, 75 both, 84–85, 143 left, 150–51, 154 bottom, 158–59

Erik Katzmaier: 111

Balthazar Korab: 161

Erik Kvalsvik: 56–57, 59, 61, 83, 92

Lilypons Water Gardens: 62–63

G. Meyers, Photo Network: 163 bottom

Karen Holsinger Mullen, Unicorn: 22 top, 76, 103, 139 top right

Oehme, van Sweden and Associates: 93 right

Shepherd Ogden: 78, 84 left, 139 bottom left

Jerry Pavia: 99 top left, 147 top left, top right, bottom left; 153 top left

Robert Perron: 66, 82, 104–5

James and Patricia Pietropaolo: 154 top

Alice M. Prescott, Unicorn: 24–25, 139 top left

Lanny Provo: 44–46, 48–49, 54, 79, 90–91, 108, 112

Jake Rajs, Tony Stone Images: 1

David Reed: 101 left

Reed Brothers: 135

Felix Rigau: 22 bottom, 124

Paul Rocheleau: 100

Andy Sacks, Tony Stone Images: 27

Chuck Schmeiser, Unicorn: 170

Charlie Schmidt, Unicorn: 50–51

Holly H. Shimizu: 10–11, 32–33, 35 bottom left

Le Spearman: 67, 136–37

Thompson and Morgan: 157 bottom, 163 top

Jay Venezia: 110

Lillian Vernon Corporation: 109

Alex Vertikoff: 38–42

Jessie Walker: 18–19, 70, 71, 128, 132

Walker and Macy: 116–17

Michael and Lois Warren, Photos Horticultural: 28 both, 29 both, 93 left, 125 both, 143 right, 144 top left and right, bottom right; 147 bottom right, 155 both, 157 top

Terry Wild: 89, 98

Lloyd Wolf: 95

index

Page numbers in italics refer to photographs. For a list of designers whose work is featured in this book, see pages 172–73.

adult garden needs, 18, 25, 104, 151
African gardens, *168–69, 169*
alphabet gardens, 23, 158–59
American Christmas Museum, *26*
American Horticultural Society, 17
animals, 20, *20*, 27, 44, 48, 62–71, 146, 148
arbors, 20, *22, 72–73*, 76, *77*, 78
Avenue A Children's Garden (New York City), *16*

bamboo, 76, 79
basketball hoops, 44, 112
bats, 64, 69
beanpole tepees, *26*, 76
beanstalks, 23, 103
bees, 27, 69
berms, 88
berries, 64, 66, 136, 144–45, 161
birdbaths, 64, *66*
birdhouses, *67*
birds, 56, 66–67
Bluemel, Kurt, 126
Bolton, Alastair, 9
bowers, *76–77*
Brayton, Thomas, 15
Brooklyn Botanic Garden, 15, 17, *88*, 94, *94, 96–97, 102*
brooks, 33, 34, *36–37, 56–57*
Brookside Gardens, 130, *131*
Burroughs garden, 160
butterflies, *13*, 68

camouflaged areas, 26, *28, 45*, 89, 112
carnivorous plants, 154, *154*
Carreiro, Joseph, 15
caterpillars, 68
Champion garden, *123*
chemicals, use in the garden, 64, 65, 106
children's gardens, public, 9, 15, 17; history of, 13–17. *See also specific gardens*
Chin, Yvonne, 38
Chinese gardens, *168*, 169
Church, Thomas, 17, 114
circular courses, 114–15
climbing, 48, 49, 96–103

climbing structures, 48, *49*, 102. *See also* play equipment, manufactured
Coe, William Robertson, 14
The Cook's Garden, *138*
Coombs School, 89
Copplestone, Nancy, 162
cottages. *See* playhouses
creatures. *See* animals
Crocker garden, 38–43

dance chimes, 113
decks, 17, 38–43
Davis garden, *148–49*
Delaney, Topher, 70
Delaney, Cochran and Castillo, 119
Denig, Nancy, 112
digging, *12*, 23, *86–87*, 89
dinosaur gardens, 23, 27, *150–51*, 151, 152–53
dirt, 20, 86–95
Duffy, Kenneth S., 56
dwarf fruit trees, 124, 142

earth berms, 88
EDAW, 100, 126, 134
enclosed spaces, 12, 72–85
espaliered trees, 124
ethnic gardens, 151, 166–69

fairy gardens, 151, 160
fences, 28, 42, 133
Filoli, *125*
fish, 65
flowers, 14–15; alphabet garden, 158–59; annual, 136, 146; attractive to bats, 69; attractive to bees, 69; attractive to birds, 66; attractive to butterflies, 68; ethnic garden, 169; fairy, 160; perennial, 26, 42, *42*, 158; performing, *154–55*, 155; perfume garden, 164–65; pickable, 21, 136, 146–47; sundial garden, 156, *157*; wildflowers, *6–7, 9, 84–85*, 148–49
forests, miniature, 20, 32–37, *56–57, 58–59*, 79
fountains, 18, *35*, 54
fragrance gardens, 164–65
Froebel, Friedrich, 14
frogs, *62–63*, 65
fruit trees, 124, *124*, 136, 142, 169
furniture, 135

gates, 132, *161*
George Washington's River Farm, *9*, 17, *52–53*, 64, 65, 69, 74, 82, *84–85, 146, 150–51, 158–59*
grasses, ornamental, 26, *28*, 42, *42*, 66, 74, *84–85*, 89, 126–27
grassy spaces, 12. *See also* lawns; grasses, ornamental
Green Animals Topiary Garden, 15
Greene, Isabelle, 38, 42, 60

habitat gardens, *8*, 27, *52–53*, 64. *See also* animals
Haden garden, *56–57*, 60, *61*, 92
health, nature's effect on, 12
heights, 20, 29, 96–103
herbs, *35*, 120–21, 136, 143, 161, 169
hideaways, 20, *22*, 72–85, 100
Hirsch, A. R., 164
Hogue, Jane, 24–25, 67, 70, 128
Hogue garden, *24–25, 67, 71, 128, 136–37*
Hotwell Primary School, 162

imagination, 18, 87, 117
indestructible plants, 27, *28*, 42, 44
insects, 65, 69
intelligence, nature's effect on, 12
intuition, 13

Jack and the Beanstalk gardens, 23, 103
Jekyll, Gertrude, 14–15
jumping, 20, 104, 113
jungle gyms, 14. *See also* play equipment, manufactured
Jungles, Raymond, 44, 46, 47, 112
Jungles-Yates garden, 44–49, *79, 90–91, 108*, 112, *112*

kindergarten, 14

Lampietti, Sheela, 68
lawns, *22*, 104–5, 106–7
learning activities, 23, 150–69
Lenox Hill playground (New York City), *16*
Lewis, Charles, 13
Little House on the Prairie (George Washington's River Farm), 82, *84–85*
local history gardens, 162
Longwood Gardens, *9*, 17, *72–73*
loose parts theory, 20, 87, 90
low-maintenance gardens, 17, 84
Lutsko, Ron, 145

make-believe, 20–21, 117–35
Marion Park (Capitol Hill, Washington, D.C.), 88
Martino, Steve, 21
Marx, Roberto Burle, 44
mazes, *116–17*, 122–23
Michaud garden, *66, 82, 104–5*
Michigan 4-H Children's Garden, 17, 103, *113, 120, 121, 127,* 134, *134,* 152, 154, 156, *156,* 161, *161,* 163, 164, *164–65*
Mitchell, Henry, 18
monkey bars, 102. *See also* play equipment, manufactured
Montessori, Maria, 117
Moore, Robin C., 29
movement, 20, 104–15

National Arboretum, *129*
National Zoo, *126–27*
nature, effects on physical and mental health, 12
natural habitat gardens, *8,* 27, *52–53,* 64. *See also* animals
New York Botanical Garden, 17 *17, 77, 140–41,* 166, *166–69*
nurture, 21, 27, 136–49

Oehme, van Sweden and Associates, *93,* 126
Ogden, Shepherd, 78, 138
orchards, 142. *See also* fruit trees
Orleans Infant School, 130, *130*
ornament, 130–31

pathways, 20, 114–15, *116–17,* 118–21, *122–23,* 126, 148
peepholes, *38–39, 133,* 134
performing plants, 154–55
perfume gardens, 164–65
pet houses, 20, 62, 70–71
Peter Rabbit gardens, 151, 161
Phipps Conservatory, 17
play equipment, manufactured, 14, *16,* 23, 102, 108
play structures, natural, 102. *See also specific types*
playgrounds, 13–14, *16*
playhouses, *14,* 14–15, 20, *26,* 82–85, 128
poisons. *See* chemicals, use in the garden; safety; toxic plants
Pollack garden, *55*
ponds, *52–53,* 55, 65

pools, 18, 33, 60–61. *See also* ponds; swimming pools
Potter, Beatrix, 161
predators, 12, 20, 72
privacy, 25, *26, 28*
public children's gardens, 9, 15, 17; history of, 13–17. *See also specific gardens*
pumpkins, *18–19, 140*

rainbow gardens, 166
Red Butte Garden, 100
Reed Brothers, 135
refuges, 20, *22,* 72–85, 100
River Farm. *See* George Washington's River Farm
Rogers, Jack, 70
running, 114
Ryton Organic Gardens, 81

safety, 27–29, 52, 55, 60, 69, 95, 97, 100, 102
St. Mark's Episcopal Church, *114*
St. Werberg's Park Nursery School, *130*
sandboxes and sandlots, 14, 20, 44, *45,* 90–93, 152, *152*
Schaal, Herb, 100, 126, 134
schoolyards, *13,* 14, 23, 89, 130
sea gardens, 162
Shimizu, Holly, 11, *33, 34, 37*
Shimizu, Osamu, 11, *33,* 59
Shimizu garden, *10–11, 30–31, 32–37, 58, 120–21*
shrubs, attractive to animals, 64; attractive to birds, 66; for camouflage, 25, *26, 133;* for fencing, 28, *29;* for hideaways, 74; for mazes, 122; for peepholes, 134; for topiary, 125
slides, 14, *38, 40,* 110–11
Stein, Sara, 62
Stevenson, Robert Louis, *1, 192*
sticks and stones, 20, 95
Story Garden, *116–17*
streams, 33, 34, *36–37,* 56–57
stress, nature's effect on, 12
sundials, 156–57
sunflowers, *2,* 103, *103,* 128–29, 151, 157
swimming pools, 44, *44–45,* 60–61
swings, 14, 17, *44–45,* 108–9

teaching gardens, 15, *140–41. See also* children's gardens, public
theme gardens, 23, 25, 70, 136, 151. *See also specific themes*

thorny plants, 28, *29*
topiary, 15, *26,* 125
tough plants, 27, *28,* 42, 44
toxic plants, 27–28, *29*
"toys," natural, 94
trampolines, 113
trapezes, 44, *44–45,* 108
treasures, natural, 94
tree houses, 20, 29, 44, *46,* 100–101
trees, for arbors, 76; for climbing, 20, 29, *42,* 96–97, 98–99; for espaliering, 124; for hiding in, 74–75; for miniature forests, 79; for willow nests, 81
Turner, Kibbe, 59

urban children, access to the outdoors, 13–14

vegetables, 14–15, 21, *72–73,* 76–77, 136, 138–41, 161, 166–69
Venus fly trap, 154, *154,* 155
Veronica's Maze, *122–23*
victory gardens, 15
vines, 23, 42, *67,* 76, *77, 78,* 84, 128, 132, *133,* 152

walkways, 20, 114–15, *116–17,* 118–21, *122–23,* 126, 140
water, effect on health, 52
water gardens, 18, *30–31, 32–37, 50–51, 52–61*
water lilies, 65
waterfalls, *32,* 33, 34, *36–37, 58, 58–59*
Waters, Alice, *138*
Watkins Elementary School, *13*
wildflowers, *6–7,* 9, *84–85, 148–49*
wildlife habitats. *See* animals; natural habitat gardens
willow, woven, 20, 76, 80–81, 89
Wizard of Oz gardens, 163
woodland gardens, 20, 32–37, *56–57, 58–59, 79, 106–7*
worms, *20*

Yates, Debra, 44, 47, 48
Yorkshire Sculpture Park, 81

zoos, petting, 20

Dedicated to my mother and father, who filled my childhood with beautiful outdoor afternoons

Printed in Singapore

Updated paperback edition published 2008 by

Timber Press, Inc.
The Haseltine Building
133 S.W. Second Avenue, Suite 450
Portland, Oregon 97204-3527, U.S.A.
www.timberpress.com

For contact information regarding editorial, marketing, sales, and distribution in the United Kingdom, see www.timberpress.co.uk.

ISBN-13: 978-0-88192-843-3

Catalog records for this book are available from the Library of Congress and the British Library.

Produced by Archetype Press, Inc.
Project Director: Diane Maddex
Editor: Gretchen Smith Mui
Designer: Robert L. Wiser

Verses are taken from poems in Robert Louis Stevenson's *A Child's Garden of Verses*, which has delighted children of all ages since 1885. Stevenson (1850–94), a Scotsman, was the author of other beloved childhood tales such as *Treasure Island* (1883) and *The Strange Case of Dr. Jekyll and Mr. Hyde* (1886).

Acknowledgments

This book could not have been completed without the help of many generous people. I especially wish to thank Jane Taylor, Catherine Eberbach, Maureen Heffernan, Mary Rivkin, Robin Moore, Susan Goltsman, Roger Hart, and Mark Francis for invaluable advice and inspiring leadership in the emerging field of public garden design for children. For horticultural and landscape design advice and for sharing memories of childhoods outdoors, I thank Kibbe Turner, Kenneth Duffy, Topher Delaney, Herb Schaal, Thomas Arnold, Emily Davidson, Andrea Lybecker, Emilie McBride, Kathy Wheeler, Alastair Bolton, Trudi Entwistle, Jo Bemis, Charles Lewis, and Chuck Flynn. For advice about plants from fairy lore, I thank Betsy Williams and Jane Hogue.

For cheerful coordination of photography and information, I am indebted to Jennifer Shively, Mary Ann Patterson, and Nancy Ross. For sharing their gardens, children, and grand-children for photography, I am grateful to Holly and Osamu Shimizu, Joyce and Jerry Sachs, Kristina and Fred Haden, Mary Lou and Don Crocker, Jane and Jack Hogue, and Debra Yates and Raymond Jungles. And for playing before cameras in public garden settings, I thank Molly Foley, Jared Utley, DeShawn Hopkins, Claire and Julia Wiggins, my own children, Ben and Kate, and the other children whose playful images enliven these pages. For a trip to England, where I found many inspiring children's gardens, I am grateful to Keith Reas.

For their creativity, vision, and patience, I am grateful to the staff at Archetype Press: Diane Maddex, Gretchen Smith Mui, Robert L. Wiser, and John Hovanec. For her horticultural editing I thank Franziska Reed Huxley, and for her research, Leslie Moushey.

Finally, to my husband, Bill, my extended family, my friends and neighbors, and my children's teachers and sitters, I offer my most heartfelt thanks for boundless nurture and support during the writing of this book and for enriching my life and the lives of my children with their presence.

Opening Photographs

Page 1: A contemplative child rests on a swing (© Jake Rajs, Tony Stone Images).
Page 2: Sunflowers never fail to attract children (© Dency Kane).
Pages 6–7: Wildflowers appeal to a child's love of color and natural bounty (© Joel Dexter, Unicorn).
Pages 30–31: The Shimizu garden in Maryland is a miniature woodland (© Roger Foley).
Pages 50–51: Water draws humans more than all other natural elements (© Charlie Schmidt, Unicorn).
Page 170: Grass adds an element of mystery to any landscape (© Chuck Schmeiser, Unicorn).

A Note on the Typography

The text typeface is Futura Book, designed by the German typographer Paul Renner in 1927–30. Futura is one of the most popular of the geometric sans-serif faces and can be found in many children's books. The display type is Adobe Garamond Italic. Numerous adaptations of this classic type by Claude Garamond have been made since its first appearance in mid-sixteenth-century France. Robert Slimbach created this 1989 version.